A Guide to Birds of San Juan Island

Also by Monika Wieland

Orca Encounters: Images of Southern Resident Killer Whales

A Guide to
Birds
of San Juan Island

By Monika Wieland

First Edition published in 2011 by
Orca Watcher
Friday Harbor, WA 98250
publisher@orcawatcher.com

Cover design: Maria Chantelle Tucker of orcagirl.com
Cover photos: Monika Wieland
Author photo: Rainer Wieland
Interior design, photos, and maps: Monika Wieland
Raven silhouette by OCAL at Clker.com

ISBN 978-0-615-54595-0
Library of Congress Control Number: 2011917500

A note on bird names

While the International Ornithological Committee rules that bird species names should be capitalized (e.g. "American Robin"), in this text I have chosen to follow the general rules of grammar in which only proper nouns are capitalized (e.g. "American robin"). The former practice is meant to help differentiate taxonomic species from descriptive phrases, but I find the latter method to be more aesthetically pleasing and consistent with other literary standards.

Acknowledgments

As much as writing is a solitary process, every author knows that putting together a book involves the help of many people.

Jason Gunter provided the spark that got this project off the ground, and helped with the early brainstorming sessions that shaped this book.

Many birdwatchers and naturalists shared information and sightings that were key to giving an accurate representation of local bird life. I am thankful for the information shared by Shona Aiken, Tom Averna, Matt Bartels, Tom Bloxton, Tim Brennan, Debra Clausen, Gayle Benton, Kathleen Foley, Phil Green, Thor Hanson, Nancy and Peter Hardy, Blake Hough, Barb Jensen, Mark Lewis, Fred Sharpe, Nan and Steve Simpson, Victoria Souze, Nancy Spaulding, Kim Sundberg, Zuiko Swann, Rick Toochin, Julie Woodruff, and Sue Vulgares.

Kari Koski and Shann Weston gave me helpful advice throughout the project.

Katie Jones, Doug McCutchen, Susan Vernon, and an anonymous reviewer provided valuable editorial comments that helped refine the text.

Chantelle Tucker designed the beautiful cover and provided essential help during the layout process.

Vera Wieland, who has always been my cheerleader, also provided her sharp editing services. Thank you, Mom.

Rainer Wieland is the person who first got me excited about birds when I was a young girl. That is a gift I will forever be thankful for. He also edited the manuscript and provided many helpful "big picture" insights. Thank you, Dad.

Keith Constable offered so much help. He has been my companion in the field on many birding excursions. He was always the first person I bounced ideas off of and he talked me through challenges as they arose. He supported me writing this book in every way. Keith, I am grateful to have you as my partner in all things.

San Juan Island Map

Numbers refer to the site guide

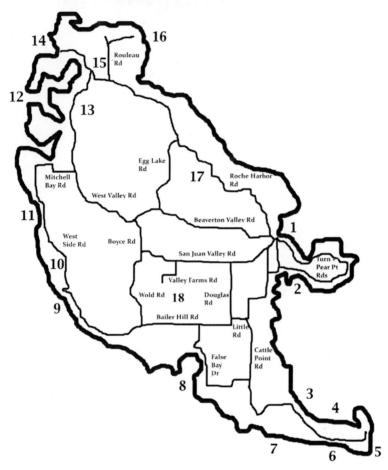

1. Friday Harbor
2. Pear Point
3. Fourth of July Beach
4. Mt. Finlayson and Lagoons
5. Cattle Point
6. South Beach
7. American Camp
8. False Bay
9. The Westside
10. Limekiln Preserve
11. San Juan County Park
12. English Camp
13. Mt Young and Mitchell Hill
14. Roche Harbor
15. Roche Harbor Trails
16. Reuben Tarte County Park
17. Sportsman's and Egg Lakes
18. Roadside birding

Table of Contents

Introduction

About 16,000 years ago, northern Washington and southern British Columbia were buried under ice. The peaks of the Cascade Mountains and the Olympic Mountains, formed by the ongoing collisions of the continental and oceanic plates, remained in the open air, but huge glaciers encompassed everything between them. These ice masses reached as far south as modern day Olympia, and near the current US-Canada border the ice was as much as a mile thick. By 12,000 years ago, these unfathomably large glaciers began to recede, helping to refine the geography of the region. The peaks and valleys of the Cascade and Olympic mountain ranges were formed, and between them deep trenches were carved out as the glaciers cleared out broken rock faults from even older tectonic events. Scattered within these newly made trenches were smaller mountains that began to rise as the weight of the ice was lifted. As the great melting continued, the trenches filled with water, and the small mountaintops became islands surrounded by a network of straits and channels that connected to the Pacific Ocean. These hundreds of islands, now an iconic part of the Washington and British Columbia landscape, were born out of the death of this ice age, and are surrounded by an inland sea.

This inland sea that took its modern day form by 10,000 years ago exists at the intersections of the Straits of Georgia and Juan de Fuca and the northern entrance to Puget Sound. For years, this diverse, trans-boundary ecosystem that encompasses the coastal waterways between northwest Washington and southwest British Columbia did not have an official name of its own. In 2009, the US Board of Geographic Names recognized a new place name that would now appear on maps: The Salish Sea. Vancouver Island and the Olympic Peninsula protect these inland waters from the open ocean.

In the middle of the Salish Sea lie the San Juan Islands. The islands are in the rain shadow of the nearby Olympic Mountains; as air rises and cools on the windward side of the mountain range, more precipitation occurs, leading the leeward side to be drier. San Juan Island itself receives only about a third to half the amount of rain as nearby places like Seattle. This results in a more arid climate than the temperate rainforest that dominates the Pacific Northwest and makes for a unique ecosystem that to some extent hosts different flora and fauna from the rest of the region. The diversity of habitat found on the 55 square miles of San Juan Island is astounding: dense coniferous forests, lively mixed woods, freshwater lakes and marshes, rural farmland, native prairies, tidal mudflats, and rocky coastlines. Altogether this makes the San Juan Islands unique among western Washington ecosystems and a fantastic place to view wildlife of all sorts, including, of course, birds. Due to the variety of habitats, it is possible to see more than 250 avian species here throughout the course of the year.

The calendar year begins in the heart of winter, a season characterized by seabirds and waterfowl. Trumpeter swans grace our inland lakes, while flocks of northern pintail, American wigeon, and other freshwater ducks congregate at seasonal ponds and marshes. On the coast, particularly at sites like Griffin Bay and off of South Beach, flocks of surf scoters and bufflehead intermix with common and Pacific loons, pelagic and double-crested cormorants, horned and red-necked grebes, and a few long-tailed ducks. Inland, mixed flocks of chestnut-backed chickadees, red-breasted nuthatches, golden-crowned kinglets, and brown creepers roam the forests.

Spring dawns early, and by mid-March change is in the air: some of our earliest arriving migrants such as tree and violet-green swallows, rufous hummingbirds, turkey vultures, and orange-crowned warblers start to be seen as the numbers of winter seabirds start to diminish. More migrants continue to arrive throughout the month of April as the waterfowl depart, and by the end of May the island's avian life is defined by bird song from the likes of the Swainson's thrush, olive-sided flycatcher, and warbling vireo.

Once we reach the height of summer in June and July, some of the world-traveling shorebirds are already heading south on their fall migration, and species such as western and least sandpipers, semipalmated plovers, and red-necked phalaropes start to show up. At sea, rhinoceros auklets, marbled murrelets, and the occasional tufted puffin continue to forage to feed their chicks, while common murre fathers will show up with fledglings still in tow. Bald eagles, which breed here in densities unmatched anywhere else in the Lower 48, also begin to take flight and new ranks of immature birds will join the distinct white-headed adults perched along the shorelines. As the days begin to shorten towards the end of August, more of our summer resident birds will begin to depart. Flycatchers, vireos, and some of the swallows will be among the first to leave.

In September, as we head towards autumn, more birds will continue to set out on migration. Warblers, as well as the American goldfinches, house wrens, and barn swallows, will be gone by the end of the month. Other migrants, such as American pipits and sanderlings, will make brief stops on their passage through. It is again the changeover season, and as the passerines head south, the ducks will begin arriving from the north. By early November, the bufflehead and trumpeter swans are once again back home on their winter waters.

Mark Lewis and Fred Sharpe wrote the quintessential account of bird watching on these islands in their 1987 book, *Birding in the San Juan Islands*. In elegant prose they guide you on a trip through all the islands' best birding hot spots and introduce you to the individual personalities of every local species. San Juan Island is part of an ever-changing environment, however, and over the course of the last quarter-century the flora and fauna have experienced changes, with the islands' bird life being no exception.

This book intends to provide an update for modern bird enthusiasts on where to go and what species they are likely to encounter on San Juan Island. Lands have been preserved and new trails developed, giving the birdwatcher more opportunities than ever to explore all of the habitats that the island has to offer. Some species have left the island: no longer do skylarks sing at American Camp, nor do parasitic jaegers regularly patrol our waterways. Instead, there are new species to seek out. Eurasian collared-doves have continued their westward expansion across the continent and reached San Juan Island in full force in 2010. The western bluebird has been reintroduced as part of a nationally recognized conservation program, and they fledge more chicks each season as a re-established breeder. Many other species have similarly increased or decreased over the last couple of decades, and those changes are accounted in this book.

The intent of this text is to provide the bird enthusiast with a reference to what birds they are likely to see on San Juan Island today in context of all the public lands available to visitors and residents alike. The information contained here is based on my experiences of birding the island over the last decade and is supplemented by the sightings and knowledge of fellow birders and by published bird reports in San Juan County. While in many cases identification tips are given relative to help the reader differentiate from other similar species seen on the island, this book is not meant to act as a field guide; rather, it should be used alongside any of the great range of field guides likely already in the library of a west coast naturalist. Similarly, while attempts have been made to include reference to historical sightings of all rare species documented in the county, it should not be assumed that this list is exhaustive. Instead, the focus of the species section is on the variety of birds you should expect to encounter with information on regional abundance and local notes of interest. The site guide section will direct you to all the publicly accessible lands that are good for birding with accompanying comments on the species most likely to be encountered at each location. My hope is that this book will help you explore the amazing variety of avian life on and around San Juan Island – enjoy!

Site Guide

How to use this section

This portion of the book gives you information about all of the publicly accessible lands on San Juan Island that are good for bird watching. This section is intended to provide you with both a list of the places to bird-watch on the island as well as a description of the sites to give you an idea of the birds you will most likely encounter there. It will also inform you of the facilities and additional activities available at each location. The numbers corresponding to each of the 18 sites refer to the map at the front of the book. Each site description begins with directions from Friday Harbor, from the previous site, or both, as appropriate. There are many free maps available in town that will provide you with a more detailed road map of the entire island.

Both major and more minor birding sites are included here. If you only have a day or two on the island, Cattle Point, American Camp, False Bay, Lime Kiln Point State Park, and English Camp are some of the best areas to explore. They are some of the main attractions on the island for the birder and non-birder alike, offering great chances for viewing a variety of wildlife as well as providing some amazing scenery and the opportunity to learn about local history. I've decided to include many additional sites, however, for those that have time to explore in depth or would like to spend some time off the beaten track.

1. Friday Harbor: The Town, The Docks, The Airport

Friday Harbor

Amenities: Lodging, gas, restaurants, restrooms, trash
Additional activities: Museums, shopping, whale watching and kayaking charters, movie theater, bowling alley

A lot of the expected urban species like pigeons, crows, house sparrows, and gulls are always in downtown Friday Harbor, and it can be worthwhile to walk the residential streets, which often yield a nice variety of other species. Dark-eyed juncos, American goldfinches, chestnut-backed chickadees, pine siskins, and Anna's and rufous hummingbirds are all regular feeder visitors, as are the predatory sharp-shinned hawks in winter. Eurasian collared-doves have been regularly seen since the beginning of 2011. The trees throughout town can host downy, hairy, and pileated woodpeckers in addition to northern flickers. More scrubby plants and bushes harbor ruby-crowned and golden-crowned kinglets, Swainson's thrushes, and a mixture of sparrow species. The author has also had luck finding more unusual species in the trees at the top of the ferry lanes, such as evening grosbeaks. The resident group of northwestern crows, which often spends time on the Courthouse lawn, can lead you to something more unusual when they are mobbing a larger bird like a great horned or barred owl (both of which have been seen perched in the tree at the center of the traffic circle at the bottom of Spring Street). The crows also harass bald eagles and the various hawk species.

The Port of Friday Harbor Docks

Amenities: Restrooms, trash/recycling, overnight moorage, seafood stand
Additional activities: Aquarium tank viewing

The docks at the Port of Friday Harbor are a great place to see many marine birds that might avoid a bigger, more industrialized harbor. Glaucous-winged gulls, belted kingfishers, double-crested cormorants, and great blue herons can be expected year-round. In the winter, species like common loons and red-breasted mergansers become regulars, as do mew gulls, bufflehead, and red-necked grebes. A good place to look for these birds is from the W Dock looking toward the shoreline, where the waters experience less boat traffic. In the summer, scan for rhinoceros auklets, pigeon guillemots, and osprey from the end of the Spring Street Landing, where the building also hosts a marine aquarium featuring the intertidal species seen underneath the docks. It is also worth walking out the M Dock, the main pier extending from the port buildings, to get views out beyond the marina. Partway down the M Dock is a floating seafood stand, where Popeye, the resident female harbor seal who is blind in one eye, tends to hang out. She has been returning to the marina for more than 15 years. From the end of M Dock you can see the breakwaters around the outer section of the marina that occasionally host roosting cormorants and gulls.

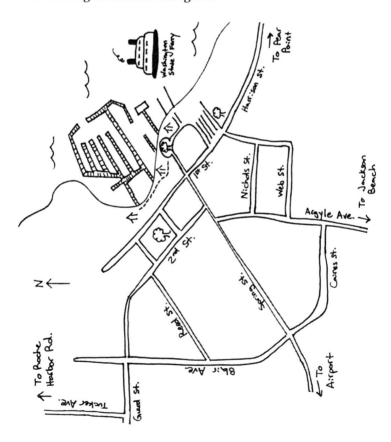

Friday Harbor: Town and Docks

The Airport Trails

Amenities: None
Additional activities: None

To reach the airport, take Spring Street 0.5 miles out of downtown Friday Harbor. To the west of the airport is a 2-mile stretch known as the Clark McAlpine Trail. The San Juan Island Trails Committee is currently working on building a network of trails that connects Friday Harbor to American Camp and Cattle Point, and this will be the start of that hike. You can access the path from multiple locations. The trailhead is near the intersection of Spring Street and Marguerite Place. You can park on Spring Street and enter the trail next to San Juan Office Supply. Alternatively, you can also turn off Spring Street onto Franklin Road (0.2 miles past Marguerite) and park at the airport, or continue and turn right onto Weber Way and park at the Skagit Valley College San Juan Center, both of which have parking lots and entrances to the trail. The final access can be reached by turning off of Cattle Point Road, which parallels the airstrip, onto Shelter Road, where there is a pullout with room enough for about three cars.

Heading from north to south, the first half-mile of the trail winds somewhat awkwardly through airport buildings and along the road. There are signs that will reassure you that you're heading in the right direction. The next section of the path past the airport terminal is paved, and it is a good place to see raptors like red-tailed hawks and bald eagles. Barn owls have occasionally been seen here, and other owl species are possible. The scrub brush on the west side of the trail is prime habitat for Cooper's and sharp-shinned hawks, as well as species like Swainson's thrushes, spotted towhees, song sparrows, white-crowned sparrows, and even California quail.

From the more open section of the path you may also spot some of the species heading to and from Jackson's Beach, such as great blue herons and various freshwater ducks. The pond visible across Cattle Point Road at the intersection with Argyle usually hosts Canada geese and American wigeon in the winter. The grassy

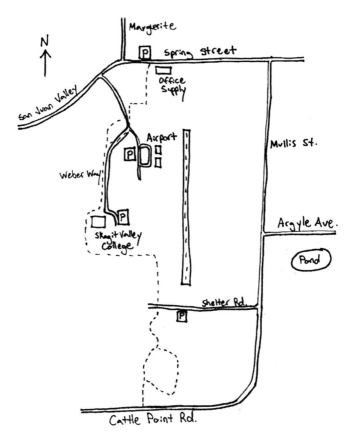

The Airport Trails

fields around the airport are a good stopover spot for flocks of American pipits during migration.

Once you reach Shelter Road you are entering a section that was newly added in 2005 and goes all the way to Cattle Point Road. This portion is more rugged and tends to get muddy in the winter and after heavy rains. Species to look for here include chestnut-backed chickadees, dark-eyed juncos, bushtits, downy woodpeckers, northern flickers, and Anna's and rufous hummingbirds. Golden-crowned sparrows are found regularly in the winter, with fox sparrows a possibility.

2. Pear Point: Turn Point County Day Park, Jackson's Beach, Gravel Pit

The 5.8-mile loop around Pear Point is popular with bike riders, joggers, and walkers, in part because of the light traffic. To start on the northern part of the loop, take Harrison Street out of Friday Harbor; it will become Turn Point Road. Alternatively, to start on the southern part of the loop, head out of downtown Friday Harbor on Spring Street. Turn left on Argyle, then after 0.75 mile turn left onto Pear Point Road. A lot of bird species can be seen and heard while traveling the road, and the following places are worthwhile stops for birders.

Turn Point County Day Park

Amenities: Bike rack, benches, kayak launch
Additional Activities: None

If you take Harrison Street out of town, 2 miles from Friday Harbor you will come to Turn Point County Day Park on Pinedrona Lane. Birders should not underestimate the importance of this tiny park, the only public access to the water along most of the Pear Point loop. From the small gravel parking area you can walk straight out to the water and look for birds along the gravel shoreline and in the protected cove between San Juan Island and Turn Island State Park just offshore. It is a good place to see Canada geese, horned and red-necked grebes, common loons, surf scoters, all three mergansers, and harlequin ducks, as well as an opportunity to scan for shorebirds along the beach in front of the private residences. The scrub brush in the area is also home to an assortment of sparrows, spotted towhees, as well as rufous hummingbirds in spring. It is a quick stop, and you never know what you might find; the author has turned up uncommon species like the black scoter here.

Jackson's Beach

Amenities: Restrooms, trash, picnic tables, fire pits, boat launch, volleyball courts
Additional Activities: Beachcombing, boating, beach volleyball

Jackson's Beach is a Port of Friday Harbor property located about 1.5 miles outside of Friday Harbor. The easiest access to the beach is to turn left on Argyle Avenue after taking Spring Street out of town. After 0.75 mile, turn left on Pear Point Road. Jackson's Beach will be 0.5 mile out this road.

Like many places on San Juan Island, Jackson's Beach hosts a diversity of habitats that make it an excellent place to bird. On one side of the spit is Griffin Bay, where you are likely to see a variety of sea birds, and on the other side is the protected Argyle Lagoon, home to an entirely different collection of species.

As you make your way down the hill at the beginning of the Jackson's Beach Road, it is tempting to start by driving all the way out to the end, however it is usually worth it to take your time. The little pocket beach at the bottom of the hill on the right-hand side often hosts a couple of shorebirds or ducks that are not seen on the main beach areas. The parking space along the left-hand side of the road will give you access to the picnic areas and if you make your way through the abundant driftwood you can walk along the beach that borders Griffin Bay. At the near end is the old gravel pit barge dock, where species like pigeon guillemots and rock pigeons are often hanging out. The little island just past the remnants of the pier is a common spot for great blue herons, and may host some rocky shorebirds distinguishable through a scope. Out in the bay itself you are likely to see the common local seabirds, as well as species such as red-necked grebes and the occasional long-tailed duck in the winter. At the far end of the beach there is often a bald eagle perched on one of the Port buildings or in the trees across the lagoon. A flock of gulls is found there year-round as well, and it is one of the best places for finding a purebred western gull among the glaucous-winged gulls and

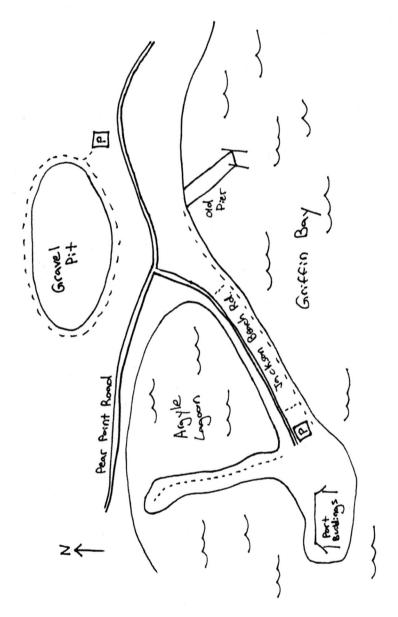

Jackson Beach and the Gravel Pit

glaucous-winged gull x western gull hybrids, which are common.

The boat launch is at the far end of Jackson's Beach Road and right next to it is a University of Washington marine research preserve. You can walk out on this gravel bar to bird Argyle Lagoon. Shorebirds such as semipalmated plovers, greater yellowlegs, and black turnstones are seen here. Migrating sandpipers may like the mud spit at the end. It is not unusual to find large congregations of killdeer camouflaged among the rocks. Bufflehead, both goldeneye species, and some freshwater duck species such as green-winged teal, gadwall, and mallards are regulars in the winter. This lagoon is home to a resident pair of belted kingfishers, and harlequin ducks can be seen year-round as well. This is one of only a few places on the island where Caspian terns are seen with any regularity, and osprey regularly come by to forage during the summer months as well. From the end of the spit, scan the deciduous trees across the way, where insect-eating species like yellow-rumped warblers can be found.

Gravel Pit

Amenities: None
Additional Activities: None

Across Pear Point Road 0.10 miles east of Jackson's Beach is a primitive parking area that provides access to the gravel pit, which was active as part of Friday Harbor Sand and Gravel Company in the 1920s and 30s and again from the 1950s until 1999. Island Rec currently owns this 55-acre plot of land, and while there are plans to develop it at some point, no details are currently in place. A flat 1.0-mile loop takes pedestrians around the edge of the gravel pit through what is slowly becoming a grassland habitat. Due to the popularity of this site to dog walkers, the birding there is not fantastic, but the walk provides nice views of north Griffin Bay and has the possibility of yielding raptors and a mixture of prairie species like savannah sparrows and American pipits.

3. Fourth of July Beach

Amenities: Restrooms, trash/recycling, bike rack, picnic tables
Additional Activities: Beachcombing

If you take Spring Street out of Friday Harbor, turn left after 0.4 mile onto Mullis Street. Mullis Street becomes Cattle Point Road after 0.7 miles. You will see the brown sign for this tucked-away beach when heading south 5.7 miles down Cattle Point Road. The habitat ranges from mixed woodlands to saltwater bay, making it a great place to see a wide variety of bird species. It is worth taking your time to explore the scrub brush that lines the road as you drive in as well as the thin forested area you pass through on one of the two short trails to the beach. You will be rewarded with an assortment of woodland passerines such as golden-crowned and white-crowned sparrows, purple and house finches, chestnut-

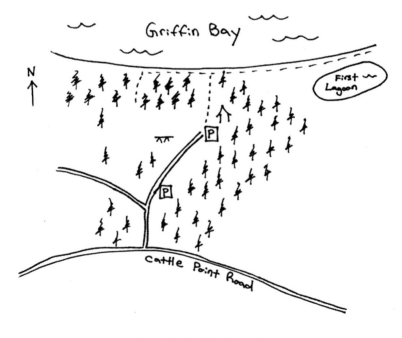

Fourth of July Beach

backed chickadees, house and Pacific wrens, golden-crowned and ruby-crowned kinglets, and bushtits. In the winter, large mixed-species flocks are common. Spotted towhees and cedar waxwings may be among the species to take advantage of the fruiting bushes. Downy woodpeckers and northern flickers can also be seen.

The beach itself stretches in either direction and provides some of the best birding access to Griffin Bay. This area is particularly busy in the winter months when common loons, surf and white-winged scoters, and bufflehead hang out along with a mixture of horned and red-necked grebes, double-crested and pelagic cormorants, and glaucous-winged, western, and mew gulls. Harlequin ducks, common goldeneye, and long-tailed ducks are also expected. During windy days even more birds from the straits take refuge here. Large mixed species flocks of gulls often pass through or follow along behind fishing vessels hoping for scraps. These feeding congregations lead to the occasional sighting of the now locally rare parasitic jaeger.

The shoreline is a good spot to look for western and least sandpipers, dunlin, sanderlings, and semipalmated and black-bellied plovers during migration. Belted kingfishers patrol regularly. The ever-present driftwood high on the narrow beach is a haunt for several sparrow species (song, white-crowned, savannah) and also provides perches for the occasional northern shrike in the winter months. If you walk east down the beach, the boggy area on your right is home to northern rough-winged swallows in the summer. A little further on, First Lagoon is also a stopover for migrating shorebirds and a refuge for flocks of freshwater ducks.

4. Mt. Finlayson and Jakle's and Third Lagoons

If you head south from Fourth of July Beach on Cattle Point Road 0.5 mile you will see a sign for the main parking area at Jakle's Lagoon on the left. There are two main routes through this network of trails: the Mt. Finlayson Trail that heads up the bluffs to the 290 foot summit, and the Lagoon Trail that descends through the woods behind the Service Road sign and heads for the two lagoons. The two paths connect, and it is 2.9 miles if you want to walk the whole loop. There is also a 1-mile nature loop trail that goes through the woods and along the grassy west side of Mt. Finlayson. A trail map is posted at the edge of the parking area so you can take a closer look at your options. From the parking area you can look down towards Fourth of July Beach. You may see some freshwater ducks or shorebirds in First Lagoon, though this lagoon is the most likely of the three to dry up in the summer.

There is another, smaller access to these trails from the very end of Cattle Point Road. Follow the road to the end towards Cape San Juan. Just before the turnaround that indicates the private marina is the trail access, and there is parking off-road for one or two cars. This is a quicker way to reach the lagoons, particularly Third Lagoon, and also avoids most of the elevation change.

Mt. Finlayson

Amenities: Trash/recycling, bike rack, trail map
Additional activities: Self-guided nature walk

If you choose to head up the Mt. Finlayson trail from the main parking area, you'll wind along the forest that borders a prairie habitat as you make your ascent. This edge habitat makes for good birding. Some woodland species to look for include Bewick's wrens, bushtits, spotted towhees, and golden-crowned kinglets. It is a great area for woodpeckers; northern flickers are common and the four other island species have a chance of being seen. On the meadow side of the trail you'll see and hear a variety of passerines, particularly savannah sparrows in the summer and possibly western meadowlarks in the winter.

Mt. Finlayson is one of the best places on San Juan Island to look for raptors. Red-tailed hawks and bald eagles nest in the trees and frequently soar on the winds that flow over the hillside. Cooper's hawks, sharp-shinned hawks, and merlins can be seen, and there is a chance for owls, particularly great

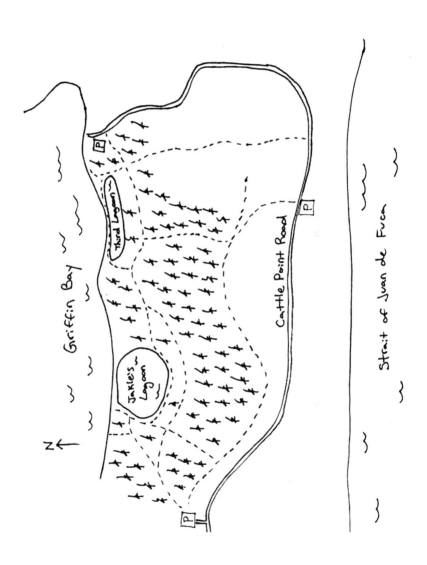

Mt. Finlayson, Jakle's Lagoon, and Third Lagoon

horned owls in the woods and short-eared owls over the prairie. Northern harriers are commonly patrolling the bluffs in the winter.

The views from Mt. Finlayson are stunning, looking across the straits over to the Olympic Mountains, but do not forget to scan the nearby treetops during your hike. In addition to the aforementioned raptors, you might find red crossbills, Eurasian collared-doves, mourning doves, band-tailed pigeons, and, in the winter, northern shrikes. This is also the most reliable spot on the island for seeing migrating mountain bluebirds.

All of the other trails lead through the dense forest, where Pacific wrens can be found year-round. Chestnut-backed chickadees and red-breasted nuthatches are common. During the appropriate seasons, look and listen for all of the flycatchers, vireos, and thrushes, as well as both kinglets and Townsend's and black-throated gray warblers.

Jakle's and Third Lagoons

Amenities: None
Additional Activities: Beachcombing

Jakle's and Third Lagoons are probably some of the least visited bird-watching sites on the island. The fact that they are tucked away makes them lesser known, but the birding opportunities here are fantastic.

Both lagoons are adjacent to Griffin Bay, where you can find most of our expected winter water species including common and Pacific loons, horned and red-necked grebes, surf and white-winged scoters, and bufflehead. The shoreline is rockier with less wrack than at Fourth of July Beach, which means these beaches attract a different variety of shorebirds during migration. Instead of peeps and plovers, look for greater and lesser yellowlegs, black turnstones, surfbirds, and both dowitchers. Black oystercatchers are present year-round.

The lagoons themselves may host some of the shorebirds attracted to mud, and also provide habitat for freshwater ducks and common and hooded mergansers in the winter. The trees bordering the inland side of the lagoons provide perches for belted kingfishers, bald eagles, and, in the summer, fly-catching passerines. Most of the larger Jakle's Lagoon is less accessible than Third Lagoon, where you can get better views (though you may have to hop over or bridge the inlet connecting the lagoon to the bay, depending on the tide and season). Third Lagoon, though smaller, also tends to host a greater variety of birds.

5. Cattle Point Lighthouse and Interpretive Area

Cattle Point Lighthouse

Amenities: Interpretive signs
Additional Activities: Tidepooling, shore-based whale watching

As Cattle Point Road nears the Cattle Point Lighthouse about 1.75 miles south of the Jakle's Lagoon parking area, there are several grassy pullouts where you can park and access paths through the meadows. The trails on the water side of the road will lead you to the lighthouse itself and along the bluffs that overlook the straits towards the Olympic Mountains. The trails on the other side of the road connect to Mt. Finlayson, Third Lagoon, and Jakle's Lagoon. This area, like so many places on the island, contains a wide variety of habitat in a relatively small space, making it a fantastic place to see a range of both terrestrial and marine wildlife.

These fields are home to a wide variety of species. In the summer you can expect to see barn, violet-green, and northern rough-winged swallows cartwheeling overhead with Vaux's swifts joining them during migration. Savannah sparrows sing all summer as well. In the winter, northern harriers make the rounds, northern shrikes may be seen perched on the bushes that dot the prairie, and flocks of western meadowlarks do their best to remain concealed among the grasses. Bald eagles and red-tailed hawks, as well as deer and red foxes, can be seen year-round.

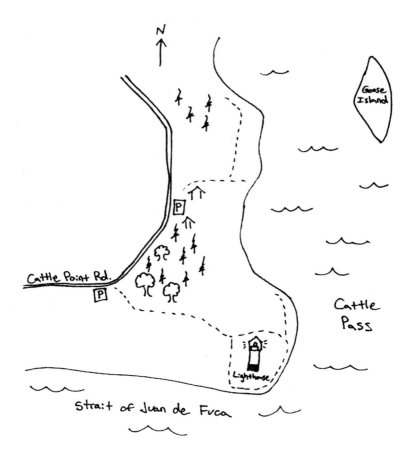

Cattle Point

As you approach the lighthouse, the thicket of trees on your left is often bustling with activity in the spring and summer. While European starlings, Eurasian collared-doves, red-winged blackbirds, brown-headed cowbirds, and house finches make up most of the cacophony, the patient observer may also find more species including black-headed or pine grosbeaks, downy woodpeckers, mourning doves, and pine siskins mixed in.

The bluffs near the Cattle Point Lighthouse offer the

best shore-based opportunity for viewing the straits and seeing some of the more pelagic species that occasionally visit San Juan County. The rocky shoreline below (the sure-footed can descend the hill in front of the lighthouse for some of the island's best tide-pooling) is a common place to see black oystercatchers and large mixed-species groups of gulls, including roosting Heermann's gulls in late summer. Black turnstones and other rocky shorebirds are also fairly common in winter. The near shore waters are a good place to see harlequin ducks, red-breasted mergansers, and pelagic cormorants, as well as harbor seals or Steller sea lions.

Further offshore are abundant feeding grounds for all sorts of marine life. This is the best place in the San Juan Islands to regularly see minke whales, a small baleen whale that feeds locally on small schooling fish. The Southern Resident Community of killer whales also spends time foraging here often between May and September, or they can be seen traveling through on their way up towards Haro Strait. A lucky observer may also be able to see a humpback whale, a species slowly becoming more common in the Salish Sea, particularly in the fall. In terms of birds, offshore bait balls are a common sight, though a scope is probably necessary to identify the species involved in these feeding frenzies. If you have one, definitely bring it, as it will give you the opportunity to see common and Pacific loons, common murres, rhinoceros auklets, and more gull species. This is also the best place to look for some of our more uncommon seabird species from shore such as tufted puffins, red-throated loons, Cassin's auklets, ancient murrelets, and long-tailed ducks, as well as our rare pelagic visitors like parasitic jaegers, sooty shearwaters, and fork-tailed storm-petrels.

Cattle Point Interpretive Area

Amenities: Restrooms, picnic tables, fresh water, interpretive signs
Additional Activities: Beachcombing, tidepooling

Just past the Cattle Point Lighthouse, 2 miles from the Jakle's Lagoon parking area, you will find a gravel parking lot for the Cattle Point Interpretive Area. This is the top spot for birding the turbulent waters of Cattle Pass, which are feeding grounds for marine mammals and numerous sea birds including all three cormorant species, common and Pacific loons, surf and white-winged scoters, horned and red-necked grebes, and an assortment of gulls. In late summer this is the best place from shore to look for the elusive tufted puffin. In addition to the coastline, the meadows here provide habitat for an array of sparrows, swallows, and the occasional raptor.

A quarter-mile offshore is Goose Island, home to roosting colonies of pelagic (south end) and double-crested (north end) cormorants. Glaucous-winged gulls and often the double-crested cormorants nest here. Canada geese and great blue herons are also common and at low tide harbor seals will often haul out on the northern shore. A little further offshore to the southeast you will see the two long, low islands of Whale Rocks just off the coast of Lopez Island. From late August through May you will see large brown Steller sea lions hauled out here, and others may be frolicking in the currents of the pass. You may also hear them roaring. Brandt's cormorants regularly roost here along with pelagic cormorants, but they are too far away to identify from shore, so you are better off searching for them feeding in the strong currents of the channel.

Walk the short path to the north along the rocky shoreline and watch for black oystercatchers and other rocky shoreline species like surfbirds. The fir trees out this way are a reliable place to see a perching bald eagle, and several pairs nest near here. Occasionally one may fly over Goose Island, creating a ruckus among the residents there.

Make sure to take the path to the end near the fence to look into the cove, one of the most reliable places on the island to see harlequin ducks and black turnstones. If you have a scope you may be able to find some of the migrating sandpiper and plover species on the far shore near the private residences.

6. South Beach

Amenities: Restrooms, trash/recycling, bike rack, picnic tables, fire pits
Additional activities: Beachcombing, shore-based whale watching, picnicking

South Beach is San Juan Island's longest publicly accessible beach, and one of the few stretches of shoreline that is partially sandy rather than rocky. To reach it, turn onto Pickett's Lane from Cattle Point Road (6.7 miles south the Mullis-Spring Street intersection or 2 miles north of the Cattle Point Interpretive Center). This short, 0.5 mile road takes you through a prairie habitat on one side, and dunes on the other. This habitat is home to a variety of small mammals, snakes, and insects, which makes it ideal hunting grounds for bald eagles, red-tailed hawks, northern harriers, and short-eared owls. Northern flickers are also common, and western meadowlarks and northern shrikes can be seen in the winter. The redoubt road that branches off from Pickett's Lane is a connection into the trails at American Camp.

From the parking areas near the water you can access an unofficial network of paths that wind through the dunes above the driftwood line. This is fragile habitat, so be mindful of where you step; there are many delicate plant species in addition to the ground-nesting birds that utilize this locale. Numerous sparrows can be seen here at the right time of year, including savannah, white-crowned, golden-crowned, song, Lincoln's, and vesper sparrows. It is also a good place to look for American goldfinches in the summer and American pipits during migration. The rare flock of migrating horned larks is also seen.

Crossing over the driftwood takes you to the beach proper, one of the best shorebird habitats on San Juan Island. Black-bellied plovers, sanderlings, and other sandpipers are most frequently encountered during both the spring and fall migration, though some may be seen in the winter as well. During the summer, Caspian terns may patrol the shoreline looking for fish, and in the fall there

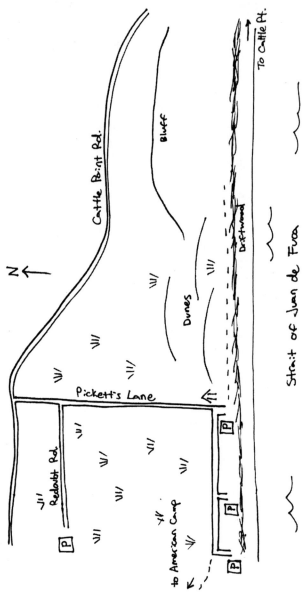

South Beach

is also a chance of seeing a migrating common tern. Large mixed-species flocks of gulls congregate here year-round, with California and Heermann's gulls occurring regularly in late summer and early fall. Glaucous-winged gulls and glaucous-winged x western hybrids are present year-round.

The beach also gives you a fantastic opportunity to check out flocks of seabirds, many of which are close enough to scan with binoculars, although a scope will probably help you identify a few more species. Early summer is the quietest time of year on the water, but during the other seasons common sightings include surf scoters, common and Pacific loons, common and red-breasted mergansers, all three cormorant species, red-necked phalaropes, common murres, rhinoceros auklets, pigeon guillemots, marbled murrelets, and horned and red-necked grebes. More uncommon local seabirds such as long-tailed ducks, tufted puffins, red-throated loons, parasitc jaegers, and eared and western grebes can sometimes be found. This is also one of your best vantage points for scanning the straits for more pelagic species that occasionally wander inland and may be visible from shore. Sooty shearwaters, northern fulmars, and black-legged kittiwakes are the most likely of these rarities.

7. American Camp and Eagle Cove

American Camp

Amenities: Restrooms, trash, bike rack, picnic tables, water fountains, interpretive signs, interpretive center
Additional Activities: Shore-based whale watching, self-guided history walk

The National Historic Park land that encompasses American Camp includes much of the Cattle Point peninsula including Mt. Finlayson and Jakle's Lagoon. This section refers to the prairie trails that can be accessed directly from the American Camp interpretive center.

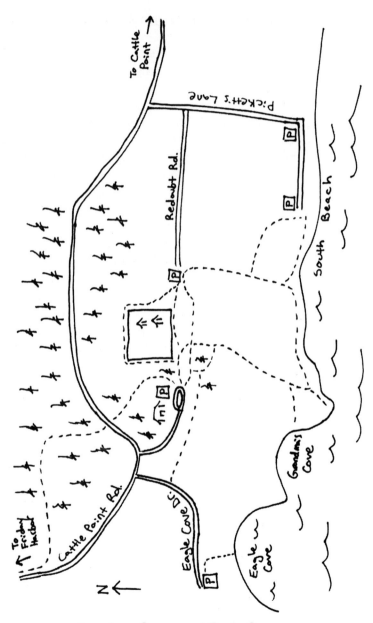

American Camp and Eagle Cove

To reach the main parking area and interpretive center, turn in after the sign on Cattle Point Road 5.25 miles south from the Mullis-Spring Street intersection in Friday Harbor (or 1.5 miles north of the South Beach turn-off). It is worth slowing down as soon as you're on the driveway to the parking area, because the forested scrub on either side of the road is usually teeming with bird life such as song sparrows, house wrens, Swainson's thrushes, and California quail. On the right side of the road as you near the parking area you can also see a bald eagle nest in the top of one of the trees. This nest was active from 1995 until 2007. While it is no longer used, there are still nesting bald eagles in the park, and the park rangers should be able to tell you where to look for an active nest.

It is also worth taking some time to bird around the parking area itself. The trees in this area are a good place to look for various warblers, rufous hummingbirds, and black-headed grosbeaks in the spring and summer, and a wide variety of songbirds at other times of year. If you want to continue to look for woodland passerines like warbling vireos, golden-crowned kinglets, and Bewick's wrens, you can follow the trail towards and then around the parade grounds. This stretch of pathway follows the edge of the woods and is prime territory for both seeing and hearing many of these and related species. Continue far enough in this direction and you'll reach the Redoubt.

The Redoubt, which can also be reached by car off Pickett Lane on the road to South Beach, provides a great overlook of the prairie habitat that park officials are working to restore to its former glory. As a result of efforts to decrease the number of introduced rabbits, many native wildflower species flourish here. The loss of rabbits has not deterred any of the predatory bird species, however; raptors such as bald eagles, red-tailed hawks, northern harriers, and short-eared owls roam here, as do northern shrikes in the winter. These birds of prey feed on the abundant smaller mammals like mice and voles, as well as snakes. A small population of Eurasian skylarks established a small population here in the 1960s after expanding from nearby Vancouver Island. Birders used to come from far and wide to see this species on San Juan Island. The skylark was last known to breed here in 1999 and there has not been a confirmed sighting in years. Instead, you have a chance to see the aerial display of a common nighthawk in the summer time, as at least one pair nests nearby.

Your other option from the parking area is to follow the trails towards the shoreline, which will take you to Grandma's Cove about a 0.5 miles from the parking area. On the way through the prairie you will pass some patches of trees and scrub brush that can turn up some interesting songbirds like migrating flycatchers (including western wood-pewees) and warblers, and Swainson's thrushes in summer. Grandma's Cove itself includes some rocky outcroppings that are great places to look for black oystercatchers and black turnstones, as well as other migrating species. The same variety of sea birds that can be seen from South Beach can be seen here, including all the loons, grebes, and scoters. You can also walk out on the headlands to the left of the cove to get a better view of the Straits. The rocks at the end of this small peninsula are a common roosting site for glaucous-winged gulls year-round and Heermann's gulls in late summer.

As you're walking through any of the trails in American Camp, you may come across a large flock of blackbirds that more likely than not is made up of European starlings, but may also contain red-winged blackbirds or brown-headed cowbirds. A variety of swallows hang out here in the summer, with barn swallows being the most abundant. Savannah sparrows are the most common species providing summer serenades from their hidden perches among the grasses, though other species are likely to be seen as well. Look for white-crowned sparrows in the summer, western meadowlarks in the winter, and American pipits during migration. The vesper sparrow, once abundant here, can still be seen in small numbers, but this ground nester has declined, probably due to the presence of feral cats in the park.

In addition to the great birding at American Camp, it is also a place to see much of the island's other wildlife. Deer and foxes are common year-round, as are seals, particularly in Grandma's Cove.

In the winter you may see a Steller sea lion offshore, and in the summer you can often see foraging orcas and minke whales a mile or more out.

Eagle Cove Beach

Amenities: Trash, bike rack
Additional activities: Beachcombing, tidepooling

When heading south on Cattle Point Road, just prior to reaching the main entrance to American Camp, take a right-hand turn onto Eagle Cove Drive. In 0.4 miles you will come to a grassy parking area on the left and the access to Eagle Cove Beach. This small pocket beach is one of the only true sandy beaches on San Juan Island, though the amount of sand exposed depends on the season and the tides. In addition to being sandy, it is a relatively protected beach, which makes it popular with waders and sun-bathers during our brief spells of warmer weather.

The short trail that takes you down to the beach parallels a creek and is surrounded by lush deciduous habitat. Look for various woodpeckers, hummingbirds, and sparrows; even the occasional great-horned owl has been spotted here. The beach itself, sandy and bordered by the rocky intertidal habitat more typical of the Islands, has potential for an assortment of shorebirds. Approach with caution, as it would be easy to flush any birds that are there; if the beach is hosting other human visitors it is unlikely much will be around. The waters of Eagle Cove are also a place to scan for many seabirds, particularly Pacific loons, pelagic cormorants, and harlequin ducks. While you're unlikely to find anything here that you will not be able to see at nearby American Camp, its remote location and comparative anonymity among visitors may make it a worthwhile stop for birders during all but the busiest days of summer.

8. False Bay and False Bay Drive

Amenities: Bench
Additional Activities: Beachcombing

To reach False Bay, take Spring Street 1.6 miles out of Friday Harbor. Turn left onto Douglas Road, which in 1.75 miles will make a right hand turn and become Bailer Hill Road. About 0.75 miles from this turn, take a left onto False Bay Drive. The parking area will be 0.8 miles down the road.

False Bay, so-named because it is a mudflat at low-tide, is a University of Washington marine biological preserve. Students and faculty from the Friday Harbor Labs use False Bay for research and training. There is a parking pullout at the north end of the bay with room for a few cars; it is easiest to park here and walk along the road. You can also access the beach by carefully climbing down the rocks. If you bring shoes or boots that you do not mind getting wet and muddy, you can walk well out onto the tidal flats at low tide.

Because of its abundant soft-bottom invertebrate life, False Bay has long been known as one of the best shorebird habitats on San Juan Island. Unfortunately it hosts fewer numbers and types of birds than it used to. This may be in part because development of San Juan Valley has led to muddy silt replacing the original sandy bottom of False Bay. Regardless, it is still a reliable spot for seeing migratory shorebirds and is one of the best bets for turning up a more unusual species like semipalmated sandpapers and marbled godwits.

Black oystercatchers are the only shorebird species expected year-round. Western and least sandpipers, sanderlings, killdeer, black-bellied plovers, semipalmated plovers, spotted sandpipers, both dowticher species, and greater and lesser yellowlegs will show up during migration. Spring migration is concentrated in April and May, while fall migration spans from July into October. Species such as black turnstones and dunlin can be seen throughout the winter in varying numbers from year to year.

While no longer the shorebird hotspot it used to be, False Bay is perhaps now better known by birders for its winter waterfowl. In winter, you're likely to find mixed flocks of northern pintail, green-winged teal, and mallards. Large groups of American wigeon are also common, with the occasional Eurasian wigeon mixed in. Diving ducks include bufflehead, common and red-breasted mergansers, and common goldeneye. There are often hundreds of ducks, though during or immediately following storms they may be entirely absent.

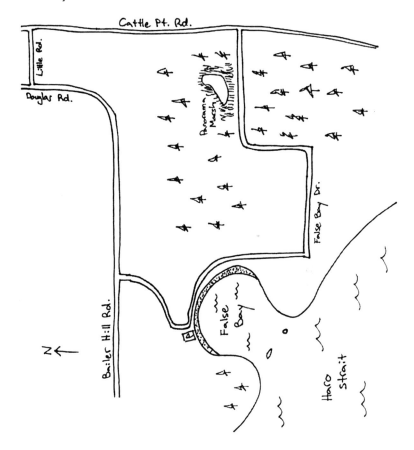

False Bay and False Bay Drive

The birding at False Bay is dramatically different depending on the tide. At high tides, the shorebird activity is pushed closer to the road, so it is possible to get good looks at any sandpipers like peeps from your car. At low tide, many of the birds out further, too far away to see unless you walk out onto the tidelands. Taking the time to explore the mudflats and tidepools can be a worthwhile endeavor. Harbor seals and sometimes orcas can be seen near the rocks and kelp beds at the mouth of the bay. Take care while exploring the sensitive marine habitat; dogs should be leashed or left behind. In addition to the amazing intertidal life, the bluffs surrounding the bay will turn up numerous raptors, belted kingfishers, and swallows such as the northern rough-winged swallows that nest near the entrance of the bay. Towards the mouth of the bay you may also find more shorebirds, and this is one of the most reliable places to find Caspian terns as they sit on the sand bars here during low tides from May through August.

Great blue herons are seen year-round. Gulls are also ever-present at False Bay, though the cast of characters changes throughout the year. Glaucous-winged gulls and small numbers of western gulls and hybrids are present year-round. A large mew gull flock that spends their winter in the bay can be seen foot-paddling in the mud, particularly during intermediate tides. Herring and Thayer's gulls may also show up in winter, while California and Heermann's gulls appear in late summer and early fall.

The trees and farmlands surrounding False Bay on False Bay Drive yield good birding, as well. Raptors ranging from bald eagles and red-tailed hawks to sharp-shinned hawks and merlins can be seen. A pair of bald eagles has nested in recent years on the west side of the bay; the nest can be seen while standing in the middle of the bay at low tide. Great horned, barred, and western-screech owls are also heard with some regularity. Groups of crows and ravens hang around, along with mixed species flocks of blackbirds. During migration American pipits like the grassland habitat, while in the winter western meadowlarks can be seen in the fields or perched on fence posts. Several pairs of reintroduced western bluebirds have nest boxes nearby and can be found during most months of the year. Depending on the season, a different mix of sparrows can be found in the scrub brush, including savannah sparrows in the summer and golden-crowned sparrows in the winter. Woodpecker species like northern flickers and pileated woodpeckers can be found on the snags along False Bay Drive.

On the north side of False Bay Drive, 0.25 miles from the intersection with Cattle Point Road, is a wetland known as Panorama Marsh. This is private land and there are no parking areas, but the road is quiet and you should be able to pull over and take a quick look at the cattail marsh, which is a relatively rare habitat to have access to on San Juan Island. As such, in addition to the more common wetland species, this is one of the only places on the island where Virginia rails and soras are regularly heard in spring. The deciduous trees between the road and the marsh are also often active with smaller birds like warbling vireos and an assortment of warblers.

9. The Westside: Land Bank Westside Preserve, Deadman Bay, and Lime Kiln Point State Park

These three nearly contiguous sites are made up of a combination of county and state park land and collectively offer the best birding access to Haro Strait. An abundance of marine life can be seen from shore here, ranging from some of the island's best tidepools, to a variety of sea birds, to marine mammals such as harbor seals, sea lions, and the Southern Resident population of killer whales (which commonly travel through the Strait from May through September). To reach these sites, take Spring Street 1.75 miles out of Friday Harbor, and turn left onto Douglas Road. Follow it as it turns into Bailer Hill Road, then West Side Road, a total of 6 miles until it opens up near the Land Bank Westside Preserve, where there are parking pull-outs. Deadman Bay is another mile further on, and Lime Kiln Point State Park 0.25 miles after that. There is a larger parking area at the state park, where a fee is required.

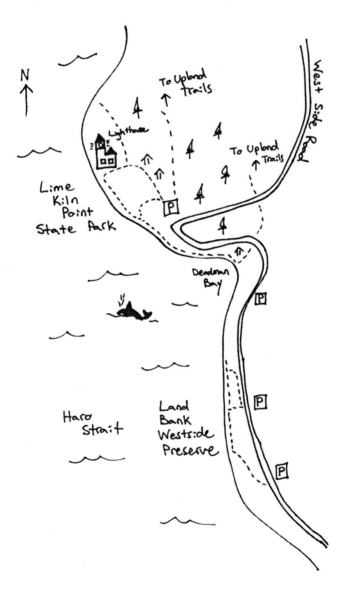

The Westside: Land Bank, Deadman Bay, and Lime Kiln

Land Bank Westside Preserve

Amenities: None
Additional Activities: Tidepooling, shore-based whale watching

Three pullouts along West Side Road provide access to the Land Bank Westside Preserve, one of the most popular properties protected by the San Juan County Land Bank. While the stunning vistas across the Straits towards Vancouver Island and the Olympic Mountains may be first to capture your attention, the hillside itself is a rich prairie ecosystem that is home to a variety of both wildflowers and birds that you may not necessarily expect to see along the shoreline. From any of the pullouts you can access the set of trails that criss-crosses the preserve. Please stay on the trails to avoid damaging the recovering prairie habitat.

Barn, violet-green, and northern rough-winged swallows dart over the grassy slope in the summertime, a time of year when white-crowned sparrows also provide a constant chorus with their singing. The occasional common nighthawk can also be seen and heard high above at dusk if you are enjoying this great sunset spot late in the day. Golden-crowned sparrows replace the white-crowned sparrows in the winter, while song sparrows and Pacific and Bewick's wrens can be seen year-round. California quail can often be heard, though finding them among the brush is a different challenge. Other more rural species like brown-headed cowbirds are also spotted, and common ravens regularly fly over from the inland hillside.

Bald eagles take advantage of the few trees that offer prime coastal perches, particularly the stand at the southern-most pullout, and an eagle can nearly always been seen on the barren snag off the point to the south. Red-tailed hawks and turkey vultures are also regular visitors.

In Haro Strait, small numbers of rhinoceros auklets, common murres, pigeon guillemots, and pelagic and double-crested cormorants may be found, or during flurries of activity such as a bait ball other species may be drawn in, including an assortment of gulls. Glaucous-winged gulls can always be observed at close range here. The bays at either end of the preserve as well as the kelp beds just offshore are likely spots for great blue herons and harlequin ducks year-round and all three merganser species in winter.

Deadman Bay

Amenities: Restrooms
Additional Activities: Beachcombing, tidepooling

On West Side Road between the Westside Scenic Preserve parking areas and Lime Kiln Point State Park's parking lot, there are a couple of pullouts on either side of the road that will give you direct access down to Deadman Bay. The bay can also be reached by a 0.3 mile trail from Lime Kiln, or from the Limekiln Preserve trails.

Deadman Bay Preserve is another property owned by the San Juan County Land Bank, and the 1600 feet of shoreline preserved here are adjacent to the state park land just to the north. Do not let the unpleasant name (referring, according to one local story, to the bodies of illegal immigrants that washed up here after being tossed overboard by smugglers in the late 1800s) keep you from visiting this scenic beach. If starting from the West Side Road pullouts, the outlet of the creek that flows from Westside Lake to Deadman Bay will be on your left. The deciduous tree stand along the creek, as well as in the brush along the first part of the trail to Lime Kiln, are good places to find passerines like Pacific-slope flycatchers, spotted towhees, and orange-crowned warblers.

The beach is busy during mid-day in the summer, since local kayak companies use it as a picnic spot for their day trips along the west side of the island. The rest of the time, however, this is one of the more secluded west side beach access points, with far less activity than the nearby Lime Kiln. Other thanb lack oystercatchers, not many shorebirds are seen here, but the shallower waters and kelp beds in the bay itself attract different sea birds than those generally seen out in the main waters of Haro

Strait. Harlequin ducks and pigeon guillemots are both more common here as a result. In the winter, bufflehead and red-breasted mergansers are expected, along with the occasional common loon and red-necked grebe. At different times of year this can be a good sight to examine numerous gull species (like glaucous-winged, mew, and Heermann's) up close. A pair of bald eagles also nests nearby, meaning they can often be seen perching in the trees or even catching fish out of the bay.

Lime Kiln Point State Park

Amenities: Restrooms, trash/recycling, benches, picnic tables, water fountains, interpretive signs, interpretive center (summer), volunteer naturalists (summer)
Additional Activities: Tidepooling, shore-based whale watching, picnicking, self-guided interpretive walk, lighthouse tours (summer)

Lime Kiln Point State Park is nicknamed Whale Watch Park and is known for being one of the best places in the world to see killer whales from shore. You do not have to head straight for the coastline to start seeing wildlife, however, as the bird life will greet you right in the wooded parking lot. Northern flickers and pileated woodpeckers can be seen and heard, and in the spring Pacific-slope and olive-sided flycatchers sing from the upper branches. House wrens nest in the area as well.

A 200-yard trail will take you straight to Lime Kiln Lighthouse, or you can follow the Shoreline Trail that winds through the woods and then approaches the lighthouse from along the coastline. Either option will take you through a mixed-forest habitat home to chestnut-backed chickadees, red-breasted nuthatches, golden-crowned kinglets, brown creepers, and dark-eyed juncos.

At low tide a couple of harbor seals might be hauled out on the rocks. This is also a good time to look for black oystercatchers, and the nimble can explore the rocks for intertidal creatures. Belted kingfishers and harlequin ducks are regular sights right along the rocks, and occasionally a peregrine falcon scouts the shoreline. A little further offshore you are likely to see a mixture of rhinoceros auklets, pelagic cormorants, common murres, and glaucous-winged gulls, with the possibility of species like red-necked grebes, Pacific loons, and marbled murrelets. Regardless of what you're looking at, the wise visitor will not leave their picnic or even their bags unattended for long. The local gangs of crows are a mischievous bunch and are expert at opening everything from zip-locked bags to backpack zippers to get at your food.

The bay just to the north of the lighthouse is home to a small nesting colony of pigeon guillemots, and your best view of them will probably be from the short path just above the lighthouse that overlooks the bay. A little further inland you can also follow a 0.2 mile trail to the restored lime kilns that are the namesake of the park, which will then connect you to the trails in Land Bank's Limekiln Preserve that are covered in the next section.

10. Land Bank's Limekiln Preserve and Westside Lake

Amenities: None
Additional activities: None

San Juan County Land Bank's Limekiln Preserve, made up of land acquired in 1997 and 2000, encompasses nearly 200 acres of mixed forest habitat adjacent to Lime Kiln Point State Park and Deadman Bay. The trail system can be accessed from either of those sites. There are also two small parking areas along West Side Road that enter directly into the trail system; they are 0.7 and 0.9 miles past the Lime Kiln Point State Park parking area. This habitat, made up primarily of Pacific madrones and Douglas fir, provides some of the best woodland birding on the island. In addition to the forest trails, there is evidence of the quarry used in the late 19th and early 20th centuries to fuel the lime kiln operation that is the namesake for this stretch of shoreline. This site provides a stunning higher elevation vista of Haro Strait.

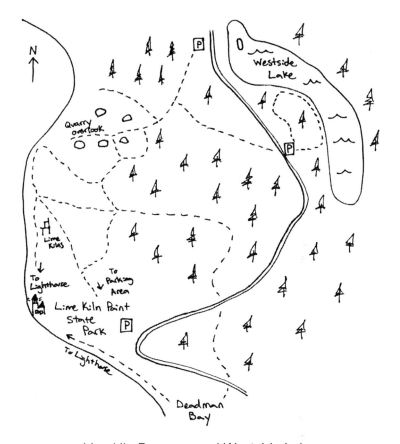

Westside Lake
Quarry overlook
Lime Kilns
To Lighthouse
To Parking Area
Lime Kiln Point State Park
To Lighthouse
Deadman Bay

Limekiln Preserve and Westside Lake

During the summer months a wide variety of birds can be heard singing here, and the patient birder may be able to find the birds themselves amongst the leaves and branches. Swainson's thrushes are the least likely to be seen, but their melodious songs are distinct. Black-headed grosbeaks, Pacific-slope flycatchers, orange-crowned warblers, Townsend's warblers, house wrens, and olive-sided flycatchers are regularly heard, and this is one of the most reliable sites on the island to find chipping sparrows. At the quarry overlook tree and violet-green swallows take flight, and there is a chance for common nighthawks at dawn and dusk.

In the winter time the bird life is different but equally diverse. Varied and hermit thrushes are common. It is likely you'll stumble upon at least one pocket of birds made up of chestnut-backed chickadees, red-breasted nuthatches, brown creepers, and golden-crowned kinglets. Fox sparrows are regularly seen as well. Throughout the year look and listen for species like the pileated woodpecker, barred owl, and red crossbill. All of these species can be elusive but this is some of the best habitat for them on the island.

Westside Lake is accessed from either of the parking areas along West Side Road. The northern parking area provides the best view of the lake, which like the woodlands supports a different cast of species depending on the season. In the winter, ring-necked ducks, lesser scaup, common mergansers, and bufflehead are the primary species seen. In the summer, this is one of the best places to find wood ducks on the island, as they regularly breed here. Hooded mergansers are the only waterfowl species to be seen on the lake year-round, and while they are generally more numerous in the winter, at least one pair has bred here for the last several years.

The deciduous scrub surrounding the lake is most active in the spring and summer, hosting species like cedar waxwings, Wilson's warblers, and yellow warblers. It is always worth taking a close look of the small island in the center of the lake to turn up these and other species.

The southern parking area leads to a loop trail that provides views of the more remote sections of the lake. While this section of trail is usually good for woodland birds, the rest of the lake is often pretty quiet, rarely turning up any species not seen from the north parking area.

11. San Juan County Park

Amenities: Restrooms, trash/recycling, bike rack, picnic tables, BBQ areas, boat and kayak launch, campground
Additional activities: Shore-based whale watching, picnicking, camping

San Juan County Park, located 2.4 miles north of Lime Kiln Point State Park on West Side Road, is the northern-most public access to Haro Strait. This 20-site campground is bustling from Memorial Day through Labor Day, but it also operates as a day use public park year-round. When you pull in to San Juan County Park off of West Side Road, there is limited parking by the main office, but the best place to park is a little further on past the group campsites adjacent to the day use area (an open area with picnic facilities) on the left.

As you pull in, the first water you come to will be Smallpox Bay, named because Native Americans who were infected with smallpox swam in the water of this shallow bay to cool their fever. Harlequin ducks, bufflehead, and similar species can be seen here in the winter, but in the summer all the kayak and boat traffic keeps the bay pretty bird free except for the occasional family of Canada geese. This is where most local companies launch their summer kayak day trips from.

From the open meadow in front of the day use parking area, you are looking out at Low Island, one of the numerous rocks designated National Wildlife Refuges throughout San Juan County. This one often hosts a pair of nesting black oystercatchers, as well as roosting glaucous-winged gulls, double-crested and pelagic cormorants, and hauled out harbor seals. It is a likely place for rocky shorebirds such as black turnstones and wandering tattlers to stop over during migration. The open meadow is also a good place to look for rufous hummingbirds and scan the nearby trees for northern flickers.

A path winds out along the forested point between the meadow and Smallpox Bay; this is prime habitat for varied, hermit, and Swainson's thrushes; downy and hairy woodpeckers; white-crowned and song sparrows; and other woodland passerines like chestnut-backed chickadees and brown creepers.

There is another small pocket beach to the north of the meadow, accessible down a flight of stairs. Bald eagles and belted kingfishers are frequently nearby, and other sea birds like rhinoceros auklets and pigeon guillemots may be spotted here as well.

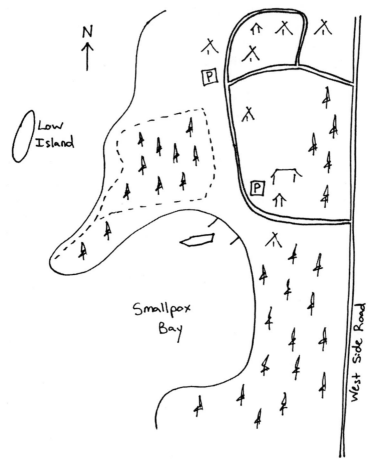

San Juan County Park

12. English Camp

Amenities: Restrooms, trash/recycling, bike racks, picnic tables, water fountain (summer), interpretive signs, interpretive center, dinghy dock
Additional Activities: Self-guided history walk

The historic site of English Camp, also known as British Camp, is primarily a mixed woodland habitat that borders Garrison Bay. Species such as pileated woodpeckers, Bewick's wrens, Pacific-slope flycatchers, common ravens, and mixed flocks of chestnut-backed chickadees, red-breasted nuthatches, brown creepers, and dark-eyed juncos can be seen throughout the site.

To reach English Camp, take 2nd Street out of Friday Harbor. Turn right on Tucker Street, which will become Roche Harbor Road after 0.3 miles. Follow it an additional 7.3 miles to where it intersects with West Valley Road. Turn left here and follow the road 1.25 miles to the English Camp entrance. As soon as you pull off of West Valley Road you will enter some of the densest forested area of English Camp, a good area to look for pileated woodpeckers. The comparatively open parking area at the end of the driveway is a place to listen and look for all our local hummingbird, vireo, and thrush species. There are multiple trails that depart from the parking lot to take you through the woods in different directions. The eastern trail will take you up the slope towards Young Hill, which also connects into Mitchell Hill and the Roche Harbor Trail system. To the north beyond the restrooms are some of the least traveled trails in the park that wind through the forest and eventually end up back at West Valley Road. The main trail, to the west, will take you down to the parade grounds, or there is a short offshoot that winds up the hill to the Officer's Quarters Site and down to the Formal Gardens. Any of these trails are great places to look for western tanagers, ruby-crowned and golden-crowned kinglets, Pacific-slope flycatchers, and all our local wood warbler species, in addition to the other passerines mentioned above.

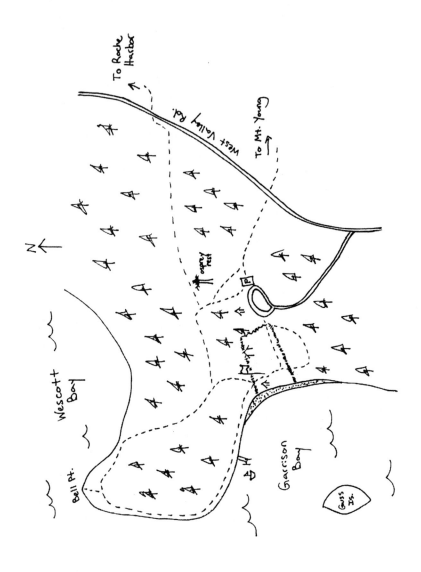

English Camp

The field that was the parade grounds for the Royal Marine Camp overlooks Garrison Bay and includes several historic buildings, one of which contains the site's visitor center. This open area is usually fairly quiet bird-wise, though barn swallows will fly overhead in summer and the field often hosts a flock of Canada geese. If the geese are not grazing in the grass, look for them over at the small Guss Island just across the way. You can also see the summer resident osprey from the parade grounds. If you stand near the flag pole and look away from the water, you'll be able to see their nest on top of a bare snag at the furthest tree line. The nest has blown down on occasion during the winter, but thus far the pair has always returned and dutifully rebuilt it. The bay itself hosts an interesting mix of both typical saltwater and freshwater species such as great blue herons, red-breasted and common mergansers, surf scoters, lesser scaup, and bufflehead depending on the season. The bay is usually busiest in the winter months.

The main hike through the Camp is the 1-mile Bell Point Loop trail. The first part of the path follows the edge of Garrison Bay, so look for black oystercatchers and belted kingfishers. Northern rough-winged swallows are typically found near the dinghy dock. The scrub on the wooded side of the trail is often an active bird area, including varied thrushes, spotted towhees, Pacific and house wrens, and the ubiquitous song sparrow.

Before the trail winds away from the water, you'll have the opportunity to walk straight out to Bell Point itself, which is the best birder's view of Westcott Bay. In addition to the ever-present double-crested cormorants on the distant dock pilings, look for red-necked grebes and other sea birds like white-winged scoters, Pacific loons, and pigeon guillemots. The osprey that nest above the parade grounds will come over here to fish. Bald eagles can be seen throughout the park, but they often perch in the trees on Bell Point, so look above you.

Back on the main trail, you will leave the water's edge and re-enter the woods. This area is a prime spot to look for band-tailed pigeons and Townsend's warblers in addition to more of the other forest species. Eventually the loop will bring you back to the parade grounds, or you can continue up to some of those lesser-used trails that will take you back to the north end of the parking lot.

13. Mt. Young and Mitchell Hill

Mt. Young

Amenities: Restrooms at English Camp parking area
Additional Activities: None

Mt. Young, also known as Young Hill, is part of the National Park land that makes up English Camp. The trail to the 650' summit begins at the east end of the English Camp parking lot. This section of the hike between the parking area and West Valley Road is an active bird area and can turn up species like western tanagers, western wood-pewees, warbling and Cassin's vireos, and downy, hairy, and pileated woodpeckers. However, hikers wishing to avoid part of the ascent can also park at one of the shallow pullouts on either side of West Valley Road where the trail crosses the street just north of the main English Camp entrance. The gate and service road signs on the uphill side of the trail will let you know you're in the right place.

Most of Mt. Young is covered in Douglas firs and Pacific madrones, with big-leafed maple, juniper, and various coniferous species mixed in. This was not always the case, though, and efforts are being undertaken to restore the Garry oak habitat that dominated part of the hillside when natives routinely burned sections of the hill. Most of the oaks are found near the English Camp cemetery about 0.1 miles up the hill from West Valley Road. While this is prime western bluebird habitat, reintroduction efforts on the island have not successfully expanded to this area just yet. Nesting boxes put out to encourage bluebirds have instead attracted primarily Pacific wrens. Other species that prefer somewhat more open habitats, such as white-crowned sparrows and house wrens, can be seen and heard in this Garry oak habitat.

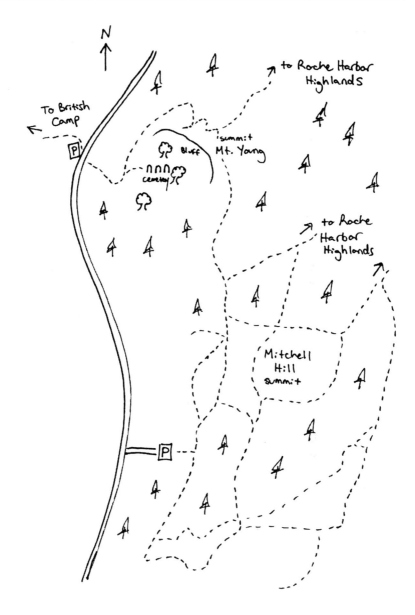

Mt. Young and Mitchell Hill

After the cemetery is the steepest section of the trail, a good place to bird by ear for species like orange-crowned, Townsend's, and black-throated gray warblers, purple finches, and olive-sided and Pacific-slope flycatchers. Hermit thrushes and Townsend's solitaires can also be found here. The first overlook you come to gives you a panoramic view of the surrounding islands to the west, making Mt. Young one of the best sunset spots on San Juan Island. Do not let the views here keep you from continuing up the trail on the left fork a little further to the summit, where a slightly different perspective awaits.

On the summit you may find yourself looking down upon soaring turkey vultures or bald eagles, and straight across at species like chipping sparrows, pine siskins, and red crossbills that are perched in the treetops. Barred owls can be heard from here and during the height of summer common nighthawks can be seen performing aerial displays up above at dusk and dawn. From the summit, a couple of unmarked trails connect to the adjacent Mitchell Hill and Roche Harbor Trail properties.

Mitchell Hill

Amenities: Trail map
Additional Activities: Trails open to mountain biking and horseback riding

Mitchell Hill, adjacent to Mt. Young and the Roche Harbor Trail systems and accesible from either one, is made up of over 300 acres. It was owned by the Department of Natural Resources until being acquired by the San Juan Island National Historic Park in late 2010. To reach Mitchell Hill directly, turn onto Horse Trail Road off of West Valley Road approximately 0.75 miles north of its intersection with Mitchell Bay Road or 0.8 miles south of the English Camp entrance. Up the hill is a small parking area with room for about three cars.

There are approximately 3 miles of trails that are part of the Mitchell Hill Property, though much longer hikes are possible since it connects with the other trail systems mentioned above. The network of trails on the 450' Mitchell Hill is complicated and the maps are incomplete, so plan to wander through rather than setting your route ahead of time. The main trails and service roads are fairly well maintained, but the single track paths can be quite muddy in places.

Like the rest of the north end of San Juan Island, the habitat here is wooded, and all of the local thrush, woodpecker, finch, wood-warbler, and flycatcher species can be found along with the ever-present chestnut-backed chickadees, red-breasted nuthatches, brown creepers, and, in winter, golden-crowned kinglets. It does tend to be a more open forest habitat than that found on the Roche Harbor Trails, however, which means in addition to many of the more common local woodland species, birds such as willow flycatchers, black-headed grosbeaks, house wrens, rufous hummingbirds, and warbling vireos may be more likely at this site.

14. Roche Harbor: The Town, The Quarry Trail, and The Mausoleum Trail

Roche Harbor, home of Roche Harbor Resort, is an upscale community at the north end of San Juan Island and a popular destination among boaters. While generally not near the top of the list of places to bird, the bustling harbor is another water access and there are a couple of interesting hikes nearby. It is especially worth a stop if you are making a tour of the whole island and want to grab a bite to eat along the way without making your way all the way back to Friday Harbor. To reach Roche Harbor directly from Friday Harbor, take 2nd Street out of town and turn right on Tucker Avenue. It will shortly become Roche Harbor Road; follow it a total of 9.3 miles to the town of Roche Harbor.

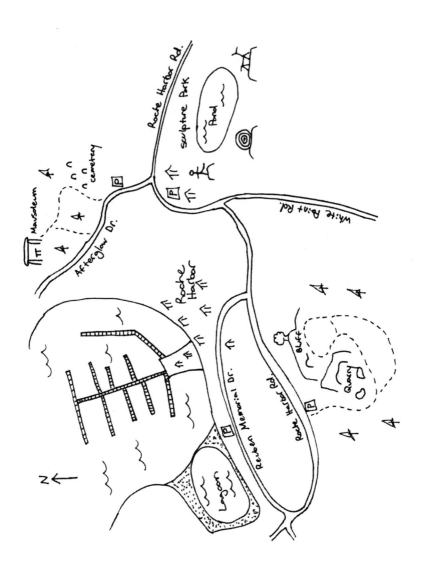

Roche Harbor

The Town

Amenities: Lodging, gas, restaurants, restrooms, trash, overnight moorage
Additional activities: Shopping, spa, whale watching and kayak charters

The small but busy village of Roche Harbor provides a surprising variety of bird habitats. The more urban setting attracts the expected rock pigeons, house sparrows, and crows, but the garden landscaping also appeals to species like rufous and Anna's hummingbirds. Walking the docks will give you a view out towards Mosquito Pass, where you may see any of a variety of seabirds including pigeon guillemots, pelagic cormorants, and surf scoters. At the south end of town is a small lagoon where great blue herons, belted kingfishers, red-breasted mergansers, and bufflehead might be found.

The Quarry Trail

Amenities: Benches
Additional activities: None

Near the very end of Roche Harbor Road, just before looping around onto the one-way Reuben Memorial Drive that takes you to the heart or Roche Harbor, there is a rustic parking area with room enough for three or four cars on the left-hand side of the road. A few wooden signs designate this as the entry to the Roche Harbor Quarry. Just like its sister site near Lime Kiln Point State Park, this quarry provided the limestone rocks that were the basis for the lime industry that was a booming business on the island in the early 1900s. The kilns themselves can be seen from the town; this trail will lead you through the quarries and up to a viewpoint looking to the northwest.

The most difficult part of the trail is at the beginning where it is steepest, narrowest, and most unstable. The habitat is stunning, winding through a rocky canyon unlike any other on the island. Migrating rock wrens occasionally stop over on San Juan Island, and this is a good place to look for one. It is no surprise that the rest of the bird life here is similar to that seen on the Limekiln Preserve near the Lime Kiln quarry. Look for an assortment of forest-dwelling species such as all the thrushes, flycatchers, wrens, finches, crossbills, and wood-warblers, in addition to the predictable dark-eyed juncos, chestnut-backed chickadees, golden-crowned kinglets, and brown creepers. Some of the more open habitats host violet-green swallows, turkey vultures, and perhaps even a common nighthawk during the height of summer. Surprisingly there are a couple of marshy ponds tucked away among the boulders, so you may come across a duck or heron, though a better opportunity for finding freshwater waterfowl in Roche Harbor is probably at the pond in the Sculpture Park on your way into town.

At the top of the trail you will find benches and a beautiful overlook of the surrounding area. You can descend the same way you came or continue on with the network of trails that will take you further back into the woods. Eventually the trails will come out on one of the nearby roads at a different spot or will loop back around to where you started.

The Mausoleum Trail

Amenities: None
Additional activities: None

The Roche Harbor Mausoleum is a memorial to the McMillins, the family that ran the Roche Harbor lime industry in the late 19th and early 20th century. To reach the monument, turn off of Roche Harbor Road onto Afterglow Drive near the Roche Harbor airport. On the right is a small parking area, and you will see a sign for The Mausoleum. (You can also access the Roche Harbor Trails from this site - look for the trailhead near the airport.) This forested trail starts by winding through a graveyard, then continues through the woods for about another quarter-mile to the Mausoleum itself (follow the "M" signs).

The largely coniferous forest found around the Mausoleum is perfect habitat for woodpeckers, so look for the hairy and pileated as well as red-breasted sapsuckers. The locally abundant woodland passerines like chestnut-backed chickadees, red-breasted nuthatches, Pacific wrens, spotted towhees, and song sparrows are common. The habitat here is a denser woodland than found on most of the rest of the island, so species like great horned owls and barred owls should be possible as well. This is a relatively small site and all species found here can readily be found elsewhere, but it is worth the visit for those who are interested in local history or are staying near Roche Harbor.

15. Roche Harbor Trails and Roche Harbor Highlands

Roche Harbor Trails

Amenities: Trash/recycling (at disc golf parking area), trail map
Additional activities: Disc golf, mountain biking and horseback riding allowed on trails

The Roche Harbor Trails, which contain more than 6 miles of hiking routes, connect directly to the Roche Harbor Highlands to the south as well as to the village of Roche Harbor to the west. There are six different parking areas that provide access to these trails. The Wescott Bay Sculpture Park and Mausoleum parking lots, both near the entrance to Roche Harbor, offer access to the trailheads for the Airport and Roche Harbor Road Trails. Along Roche Harbor Road are two more small parking areas at the water treatment plant (8.5 miles from Friday Harbor) and near the intersection with West Valley Road (7.75 miles from Friday Harbor), and these link directly into the Forest Glen Loop and Wetlands Loop. Finally, the Rouleau Road Trail can be accessed by turning right onto Rouleau Road 7.25 miles out Roche Harbor Road from Friday Harbor. The parking lot at the disc golf course 0.9 miles out Rouleau Road on the left provides access, as does a small pullout 0.1

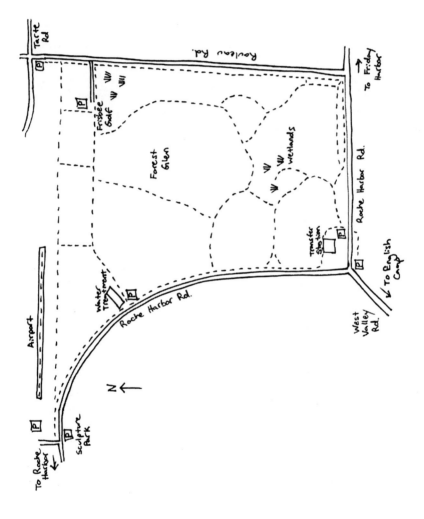

Roche Harbor Trails

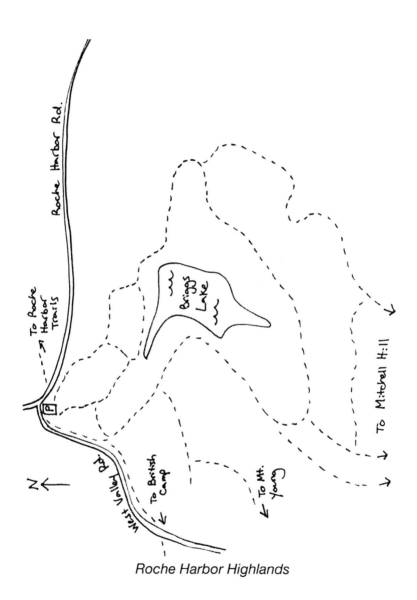

Roche Harbor Highlands

miles further on at the intersection of Rouleau Road with Tarte and Limestone Point Roads.

The southern portion of these trails, particularly near the Wetlands Loop, are notoriously muddy for much of the year, so you will want mud boots in the fall, winter, or spring to explore this section. Boardwalks are built over the wettest sections of these rustic trails. That said, the woodlands that these trails wind through are well worth the visit, being perhaps one of the most consistent places for large woodland flocks of multiple species. Chestnut-backed chickadees, red-breasted nuthatches, ruby-crowned and golden-crowned kinglets, and dark-eyed juncos can be found throughout the island, but rarely in the numbers that are found on the Wetland and Forest Glen Loop trails.

The Roche Harbor Trails are perhaps also one of the best places to bird by ear, particularly in the spring. The diversity of species found here is impressive, but it often takes patience to locate the birds among the trees and shrubs. In addition to the species mentioned above, yellow-rumped and orange-crowned warblers, purple finches, house and Pacific wrens, and all our flycatchers and woodpeckers are also regularly heard singing or calling.

The Airport, Roche Harbor Road, and Rouleau Road trails that skirt this property are prime edge habitats. Rufous hummingbirds are abundant in spring. Some areas overlook more rural habitat where common ravens, bald eagles, and turkey vultures are regularly sighted.

Roche Harbor Highlands

Amenities: Trail map
Additional Activities: Mountain biking and horseback riding allowed on trails

The best access to the Roche Harbor Highland trails is at the corner of Roche Harbor and West Valley Roads where there is a small gravel parking lot 7.75 miles out Roche Harbor Road from Friday Harbor. You can pick up a map at one of the trailheads, which will help to guide you through the complicated network of more than ten miles of trails that connect to English Camp, Mount Young, and Mitchell Hill. Across the street you can also access the Roche Harbor Trails.

The majority of the paths take you through the forest, where at times it seems there is a total absence of birds until you come across a pocket of activity often made up of our most abundant woodland residents. Throughout much of the year common ravens provide a soundtrack to your hike. These trails are also a good place to look for varied and hermit thrushes, Pacific and Bewick's wrens, hairy and pileated woodpeckers, and various species of flycatchers and warblers. The trails are wide, but be aware that they can get quite muddy after heavy rains.

One of the major birding highlights of the Roche Harbor Highlands is the Briggs Lake reservoir, which is one of the largest lakes on the island. While the Lake Loop trail takes you around the circumference of the lake, the water is often hidden from view. The best birding access is near the dam at the north end of the lake, where you can walk out on the grassy hillside to get a good look at the water. (Visitors are asked to do their part to protect the water quality of this reservoir, so please stay out of the water and take other appropriate precautions.) A variety of ducks stop over here, with bufflehead and ring-necked ducks being particularly common in the winter. Common mergansers, double-crested cormorants, and pied-billed grebes also hang out here, with red-winged blackbirds liking the cattail edges of the lake. Bald eagles and osprey might be seen as well.

16. Reuben Tarte County Park

Amenities: Trash, restrooms, benches
Additional activities: None

This small, tucked away park is little visited, but yields the only public access to the northeast coast of the island which provides dramatic views overlooking northern San Juan Channel. You reach

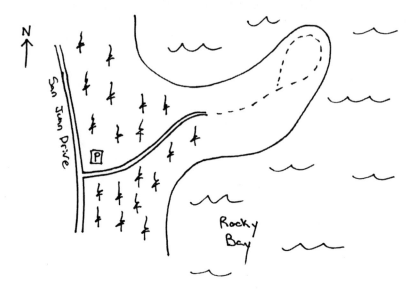

Reuben Tarte County Park

this park off of Roche Harbor Road; start by following it 7.25 miles out of Friday Harbor. Take a right on Rouleau Road and follow it exactly 1 mile to the first intersection, where you will take a right on Limestone Point Road. Follow this until it makes a "T" in 0.8 miles, where you will turn right on San Juan Drive. In 0.3 miles you will come to a parking area on the left with a wooden sign for Reuben Tarte Memorial Park. There is a steep driveway that takes you down to the park itself where there is limited parking and unloading room.

On either side of the bluff are two picturesque pocket beaches that may host visiting shorebirds from time to time, particularly during lower tides when the rocks are exposed. To the south you can see O'Neal Island in Rocky Bay, which is often home to a nesting pair of bald eagles. A nest is visible in the tallest tree in the center of the island. You can walk several hundred feet out on the bluff to overlook the water to the northeast. The confluence of water channels here makes for complex currents that attract a lot of marine life. A variety of gulls, common murres, pelagic cormorants, pigeon guillemots, and marbled murrelets can be seen here year-round. This is one of the most likely places to see Bonaparte's gulls from shore; look for them during migration. Common loons and other sea ducks are also possible. In addition to marine birds, harbor seals, harbor porpoise, and Steller sea lions are regularly seen.

17. Sportsman's and Egg Lakes
Sportsman's Lake

Amenities: Boat launch
Additional activities: Boating (no motors), fishing

3.6 miles north of Friday Harbor out Roche Harbor Road is Sportsman's Lake. There is a small public access to the lake best identified by a widening in the road where several cars can park, as well as a downhill access to the small boat ramp. The shoulder of Roche Harbor Road is wide enough here to walk north of the parking area to see the lake. Look for the tree that hosts roosting double-crested cormorants year round. To get the best views of the central and southern portions of the lake, walk down the boat ramp or out onto the knoll that gives you a panoramic view of the water.

In the winter, this is where the largest concentrations of trumpeter swans are usually seen, along with flocks of bufflehead, ring-necked ducks, and common mergansers. It is also one of the best places to look for most other freshwater waterfowl; many of the duck species can be seen elsewhere on the island in some of the smaller lakes and ponds, but a wider variety is more likely to congregate on this large body of water. Scan the edges of the lake closely to find some of them when the main body of the lake looks empty.

In the summer, all the local species of swallows can be seen here. Violet-green swallows are the most common, but tree and northern rough-winged swallows are usually mixed in. Yellow-rumped warblers and common yellowthroats can be heard singing along with marsh wrens. Other species such as cedar waxwings, spotted towhees, and pine siskins can sometimes be seen among the scrub brush.

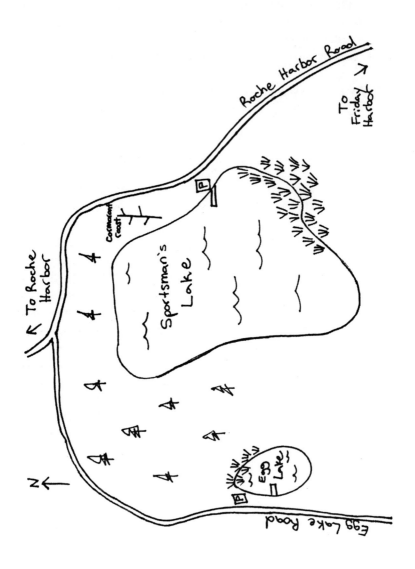

Sportsman's and Egg Lakes

Egg Lake

Amenities: Dock
Additional activities: Boating (no motors), fishing

From Sportsman Lake, travel 0.5 miles north on Roche Harbor Road before taking a left onto Egg Lake Road. Follow Egg Lake Road 0.6 miles to a gravel pullout that gives you access to Egg Lake itself. This is one of the most accessible marshy habitats on the island, as many others are on private property or fail to have parking pull-outs. Egg Lake hosts a variety of over-wintering waterfowl such as bufflehead, ring-necked ducks, and trumpeter swans. Please be especially mindful of the swans; they depart from this and other freshwater areas if approached too closely.

The habitat transforms in the spring, when many insect-eating species like violet-green swallows, yellow and Wilson's warblers, Pacific-slope and olive-sided flycatchers, and warbling vireos arrive, some of whom will stay for the summer. The cattail edges of the lake are popular with red-winged blackbirds, marsh wrens, and common yellowthroats, and elusive species such as the Virginia rail and sora may be heard here in the spring. Scan the edges of the lake for pied-billed grebes, hooded mergansers, and wood ducks. The trees surrounding the lake are a good place to look for any of our woodpeckers.

18. Roadside Birding

There are so many great places to hike around the island, but great birding can also be done from the car. In fact, much of the more agricultural habitat and freshwater marshland is best viewed from alongside the roads. This section focuses on the main roads that you are likely to traverse anyway as you head to other great birding sites, and also mentions a few side roads known for good birding that you may not otherwise visit.

Roche Harbor Road and White Point Road

As soon as the habitat opens up as you leave Friday Harbor on Roche Harbor Road, you will be passing Beaverton Marsh on your left. This conservation easement is owned by the San Juan County Land Bank, and they are working to remove non-native species and restore the marsh. Their efforts will improve the habitat for birds, particularly over-wintering waterfowl. While there is currently no public access to the land here, it may be worth pulling over on a side street and taking a look for ducks, geese, and swans.

Continuing on to the north, you will drive through rural farmlands. Some of these fields experience seasonal flooding and will host some winter waterfowl species like bufflehead and northern pintail. In the summer this is a great part of the island to find all five of our swallows species. Various raptors and owls can also be sighted here. In addition to Sportsman's Lake, you will pass some larger bodies of water near Lakedale Resort. These ponds and lakes support trumpeter swans and bufflehead in the winter, and Canada geese and hooded mergansers year-round.

At the end of Roche Harbor Road as you approach Roche Harbor you can take the left fork onto White Point Road, which will loop through residential areas and come back around on the far side of Roche Harbor. It is worth following this route at least to the intersection of Armadale Road, where a salt marsh and mud flat habitat exists. Both freshwater and sea ducks can be seen here, and it is an environment that makes a good stopover site for migrating shorebirds.

Beaverton Valley and West Valley Roads

Take Guard Street out of Friday Harbor and it becomes Beaverton Valley Road. On the right-hand side of the road about 0.25 mile outside of town are fields that experience seasonal flooding, making great habitat for large flocks of ducks during the winter months. Usually the most abundant species seen here is the northern pintail numbering in the hundreds. Unfortunately there are no great pullouts for scanning this marshy area. Further out Beaverton Valley, particularly just after the intersection with Egg Lake Road, are other lakes and ponds on private property that can be scanned from the roadside. American wigeon are abundant here and Eurasian wigeon can be found as well. Other species to look for include pied-billed grebes, gadwall, and green-winged teal. The wider shoulder makes it possible to pull over and scan here.

After the intersection with Boyce Road 3.5 miles outside of town, Beaverton Valley becomes West Valley Road. The road winds along Cady Mountain and past Lawson Lake. This larger lake for some reason tends to be much quieter than most other freshwater habitats on the island. Sometimes it hosts small numbers of ring-necked ducks, lesser scaup, and common mergansers, but other species only occur occasionally. It is tempting to use the nearby pullouts, but please be respectful of this private property.

Before West Valley Road passes the alpaca farm and approaches English Camp you will see several ponds on the left-hand side of the road. Unlike Lawson Lake, these are thriving habitats for all species of waterfowl and swallows. The largest of the lakes in particular seems to be a popular site for migrating geese. Look for the common Canada goose but also cackling geese, snow geese, and greater white-fronted geese stopping over during migration.

Wold Road

There are several small ponds and lakes along Wold and Boyce Roads that are good places to look for ducks, geese, and swans. The best spot is the lake right across from the Lavender Farm on Wold Road, which is a reliably productive birding area. In the winter it plays host to ring-necked ducks, lesser scaup, and common mergansers. In the summer all types of swallows can be seen feeding on insects over the water, and the wooded area bordering the lake is a great spot to see and hear cedar waxwings and various flycatcher and warbler species.

San Juan Valley and Valley Farms Road

As you take Spring Street straight out of Friday Harbor it becomes San Juan Valley Road. Just after the first bend in the road near Trumpeter Way (about 1.4 miles from downtown Friday Harbor) is a marshland known informally as Swan Valley Wetlands. This marsh floods in the winter and hosts all the regional waterfowl species including northern shoveler, ring-necked ducks, American wigeon, bufflehead, and northern pintail. Much of the water drains in the spring but sometimes enough remains for a few pairs of ducks (usually mallards) or Canada geese to breed. Rarer species like cinnamon teal have also been seen here. It is prime habitat for hearing Virginia rails, sora, marsh wrens, winnowing Wilson's snipe, and occasionally great horned and barn owls. Red-winged blackbirds, Brewer's blackbirds, and brown-headed cowbirds all breed nearby, as do violet-green swallows, barn swallows, and American goldfinches.

San Juan Valley Road continues through farmland where many of the more rural species like turkey vultures and western meadowlarks can be found at the right time of year. The highlight of this road is near its intersection with Wold Road 4.25 miles outside of Friday Harbor, where the San Juan County Land Bank's King Sisters Property sports a new roadside trail that allows walkers to take in the countryside. This provides a nice way to explore this habitat without being confined to the car.

Valley Farms Road, which heads south from San Juan Valley Road 2.8 miles west of Friday Harbor, is an out-of-the-way dead end road that is popular with birders in part because its rural Garry oak habitat makes it a prime place to look for the reintroduced western bluebird. The scrub brush bordering the road is a gold mine for sparrows, with all the common local species being regularly seen; in addition, some of the rarer species, like the vesper sparrow, occasionally make an appearance. The farm fields on either side of the road can turn muddy, creating some prime habitat for migrating shorebirds or over-wintering dunlin.

Douglas and Bailer Hill Roads

Douglas and Bailer Hill Roads provide one of the author's favorite stretches of roadside birding on the island, in part because of the wide variety of birds that can be seen. Various raptor species can be seen here, with species like sharp-shinned hawks occasionally swooping across the road. A pair of bald eagles is regularly seen perched in the tall tree at the 90-degree turn where Douglas and Bailer Hill intersect, or on top of one the power line poles. The power lines are also prime perches for a variety of species including western bluebirds, Brewer's blackbirds, and Eurasian collared-doves. The seasonally flooded farm fields host duck species like American wigeon and northern pintail. In the summer, barn swallows and turkey vultures are common sights, while western meadowlarks may be seen on the fence posts in the winter.

West Side and Mitchell Bay Roads and Snug Harbor

When Bailer Hill Road reaches the west side of San Juan Island, it becomes West Side Road and for a short stretch follows right alongside Haro Strait. Here is where you will find accesses to Land Bank West Side Preserve, Deadman Bay, and Lime Kiln Point State Park. After the State Park the road winds up into the trees where you will also find parking areas for Limekiln Preserve and Westside Lake. The great birding habitat continues even after these public lands end. Several marshy areas right next to the road are regular places to see wood ducks and hooded mergansers. Barred owls have also been reported here, and other owl species should be considered a real possibility.

You will pass San Juan County Park, another public access to Haro Strait. Further on, where the road takes a 90 degree turn and becomes Mitchell Bay Road, if you head left instead of right you will come to Snug Harbor. This tucked away marina is home of a small resort, campground, and general store. Snug Harbor is worth a stop just to walk the docks. The rocky outcroppings in the bay are a regular spot to see black oystercatchers, and other species like black turnstones are possible. Belted kingfishers and bald eagles regularly perch along the shoreline. The bay itself is a great spot to view red-breasted and hooded mergansers, bufflehead, common and Barrow's goldeneye, and harlequin ducks. The author has also seen species such as western tanagers and pileated woodpeckers in the trees near the campground.

Back out on the road, Mitchell Bay Road will eventually intersect with West Valley Road, but before that it will again pass a series of ponds. Unlike the more densely forested habitat along West Side Road, the water along Mitchell Bay Road is more open and as a result hosts species such as American wigeon, gadwall, and northern pintail

Cattle Point Road

There are so many prime birding stops along Cattle Point Road that it is likely you will travel this route at least once. As Mullis Street becomes Cattle Point Road leaving town, you will pass the airport where the open grasslands are good habitat for raptors and migrating species like American pipits. The road goes through a more agricultural area where turkey vultures and barn owls are regularly spotted. As the road approaches the southern end of the island it winds above South Beach and along Mt. Finlayson, providing one of the most amazing vistas from the island looking towards the Olympic Mountains. Northern harriers, northern shrikes, short-eared owls, red-tailed hawks, and bald eagles can all be seen from this portion of the road.

One of the newest trail systems on San Juan Island also occurs along Cattle Point Road. The San Juan Island Trails Committee is in the process of creating a walking trail that will connect Friday Harbor to Cattle Point. The trail begins with the Airport Trails in town, and will eventually connect to existing trails at American Camp. A section just north of American Camp, accessible from the interpretive center, has opened up on the San Juan County Land Bank's Frazer Homestead Preserve property.

Species Guide

How to use this section

The main purpose of this guide is to give you an idea of the species you are likely to encounter on San Juan Island. Species are listed in the taxonomic order designated by the American Ornithologists' Union (as of the 52nd supplement published in 2011), and every species expected in San Juan County on at least an occasional basis is listed with its regionally relevant information. I envision there being three different ways to use this section:

1. Read through to get an idea of the birds that occur on San Juan Island
2. Accompany your field guide to identify what bird you saw (e.g., if you see a hawk at American Camp and you're not sure what it is, you can use the "Raptors" section to narrow down what the likely options are)
3. Help you locate particular species of interest (e.g., if you are particularly interested in finding a rhinoceros auklet, reading that species' account in this section will tell you where and when you will have the best chance of seeing one).

In the interest of completeness, I have also included "very rare" lists of species at the end of each taxonomic section. These sections include birds that have only had one or a few confirmed sightings in San Juan County or those species that are considered hypothetical but likely to be documented at some point. Some species that have been reported in the past, for example in the collaborative accounts in Lewis and Sharpe 1987, but were subsequently rejected by the Washington Bird Records Committee or remain hypothetical, have not been included here. Additionally, introduced species that have since been extirpated are not included in their entirety. As a result, this species list is not exhaustive for every bird reported San Juan County, but it fulfills its role of giving you, the bird enthusiast, an idea of species expected to occur here, as well as a list of rarer species that have been documented over the last couple of decades.

Every species is given an abundance rating that applies to the particular habitat and season in which that species is expected. The abundance ratings are defined as follows:

Abundant – Expected on every visit to suitable habitat and usually many individuals are seen

Common – Likely on every visit to suitable habitat in small groups or as individuals

Uncommon – Expected but not regularly seen due either to low numbers or elusive behavior

Rare – Usually seen at least once per season, but may be missed in any given year

Occasional - Not seen every year due to being outside its normal range or due to irruptive behavior

Each species is listed as occurring either during summer, winter, migration, or year-round. These designations don't refer to a particular set of months across all species, but to the appropriate time of year for the given species. For example, violet-green swallows tend to arrive in March, while Wilson's warblers don't usually arrive until early May, but both are listed as summer residents. Species that are seen in summer or winter are also seen, sometimes in greater numbers, during migration, but migration is only given as a designation if that is the only time that species is seen. If a species is only seen during migration the months in which it migrates are indicated in the notes.

The sites that are listed for each species are not comprehensive, but rather indicate the few sites where you are likely to have the best luck finding that particular species based on my experience. If only a specific portion of a site is relevant, an additional notation will be made in parenthesis – e.g., "The Westside (Land Bank)". Additional regionally relevant information can be found in the notes section.

Geese and Swans

Greater white-fronted goose
Anser albifrons
Rare
Migration
Sites: English Camp, Sportsman's and Egg Lakes, Roadside birding
Notes: Most of the Pacific population of greater white-fronted geese winter in central Oregon or further south and make a nearly non-stop migration from their Arctic breeding grounds. As a result, this species isn't common here, and is usually seen flying overhead or making a short stopover during migration. Look for them in April-May and September-October.

Snow goose
Chen caerulescens
Rare
Migration
Sites: English Camp, Roadside birding
Notes: In the nearby Skagit River and Fraser River Valleys on the mainland birders can see winter flocks of thousands of snow geese, but this is one spectacle not seen on San Juan Island. Migrating birds can sometimes be seen as they fly by, primarily in March-April and October-November. Occasionally small flocks will land for a short stopover, but they don't stay.

Brant
Branta bernicla
Uncommon
Migration
Sites: Jackson's Beach, False Bay, The Westside
Notes: Unlike our other geese, the brant is associated with saltwater rather than freshwater. Not as many brant overwinter in the Salish Sea as in years past, probably due to the decrease in the eelgrass beds that they prefer to feed on, though they do still use nearby habitats. The gray morph over-winters in Samish Bay and Padilla

Bay, while the black morph is common near Dungeness Spit. They are most often seen in the San Juan Islands during migration in places like Haro Strait, so look for them in November-December and again from February-April. You can also find them near the ferry landing in Anacortes.

Cackling goose
Branta hutchinsii
Rare
Migration
Sites: Roadside birding
Notes: The cackling goose, formerly considered a small race of the highly variable Canada goose, looks like its larger cousin in miniature. In addition to the size difference, their vocalizations are a higher pitched "cackling" rather than the lower honking of the Canada goose. The Pacific coast population of cacklers summers in Alaska and over-winters in California, the Willamette Valley in Oregon, and southwest Washington, so they are usually only seen

Canada goose

in northern Washington during migration. They are early migrants, starting to head south by the end of August, and returning north as soon as late January.

Canada goose
Branta canadensis
Common
Year-round
Sites: Cattle Point, English Camp, Roadside birding
Notes: This species is more abundant in large winter flocks, particularly in farm fields and roadside lakes, but some breeding pairs remain during the summer at places like English Camp and Goose Island near Cattle Point.

Mute swan
Cygnus olor
Occasional
Sites: Roche Harbor, Sportsman's and Egg Lakes
Notes: This introduced species is more common on the east coast of the US and around the Great Lakes, but there is a small resident Pacific Northwest population of several hundred birds. Most of these swans reside along southeast Vancouver Island, but they scatter throughout Washington and Oregon and are only sporadically seen in the San Juan Islands. The Washington Department of Fish and Wildlife has an active removal program in place for this species, which has kept them from becoming more established.

Trumpeter swan
Cygnus buccinator
Common
Winter
Sites: Sportsman's and Egg Lakes, Roadside birding
Notes: Since being hunted nearly to extinction, the trumpeter swans have made an amazing recovery and returned to wintering in the San Juan Islands in the 1970s. At least several dozen birds can

be regularly seen on the lakes and farm fields here throughout the winter. Numbers begin to dwindle throughout April, though birds have been recorded here as late as June (*WOS News* 109). When viewing this species, please keep in mind that they are skittish, and may leave certain areas entirely if disturbed.

Tundra swan
Cygnus columbianus
Occasional
Migration
Sites: Sportsman's and Egg Lakes, Roadside birding
Notes: A common species on the mainland of Washington, most tundra swans bypass the San Juan Islands, so they are most likely to be seen flying overhead during migration in March and November. Vocalizations given in flight can help distinguish them from the similar trumpeter swan.

Wood duck

Ducks

Wood duck
Aix sponsa
Uncommon
Year-round
Sites: Westside Lake, Sportsman's and Egg Lakes, Roadside birding
Notes: This is one of the few ducks that is more often seen locally in the summer than the winter. They breed here in several locations and mothers with ducklings are an expected sight on many small lakes and ponds. By the end of September, most will have migrated for the winter.

Gadwall
Anas strepera
Common
Winter
Sites: Jackson's Beach, Fourth of July Beach, Roadside birding
Notes: Gadwall have interesting breeding habits. Pair bonds can develop in late fall, up to 5 months before breeding actually occurs. Then, the pair separates after the eggs are laid, with females doing all the incubating and parental care and males forming their own separate loose flocks. This helps explain why gadwall often aren't seen in great numbers, even during the winter: males get protective of their females, and often you'll only see two ducks at a time. This species has been increasing in western Washington since the 1950s and nationally since the 1980s.

Eurasian wigeon
Anas penelope
Uncommon
Winter
Sites: False Bay, Roadside birding
Notes: Eurasian wigeon are somewhat regular accidental visitors that occur all along the west coast, but they seem to occur more often in western Washington than elsewhere in the Lower 48. They

are usually found mixed in with flocks of American wigeon, though they part from them in the spring and head back to Siberia. Locally, they are most likely to be seen in the large flocks that winter at False Bay. Hybrids with American wigeon can also occur.

American wigeon
Anas americana
Abundant
Winter
Sites: False Bay, Sportsman's and Egg Lakes, Roadside birding
Notes: The Pacific Northwest hosts some of the largest wintering flocks of this species, which has been experiencing a population increase from the mid-1990s. On San Juan Island, flocks are most commonly seen on False Bay and near roadside ponds during the winter. Unlike most other dabbling ducks, wigeon are proficient walkers on land, so they are the most common duck to be seen in fields alongside geese. A few pairs may breed here, but in very small numbers.

Mallard
Anas platyrhynchos
Common
Year-round
Sites: Jackson's Beach, Fourth of July Beach, False Bay, Roadside birding
Notes: While not nearly as abundant on San Juan Island as elsewhere in Washington, this species is still regularly seen in expected habitats throughout the year.

Blue-winged teal
Anas discors
Rare
Summer
Sites: Third and Jakle's Lagoons, Sportsman's and Egg Lakes, Roadside birding
Notes: While blue-winged teal are known to breed in Puget Sound

and have been recorded nesting on San Juan Island, they are not often encountered here. Overall, the population has experienced several major fluctuations during the last 50 years, due mostly to the presence or absence of sufficient water levels in their prairie breeding grounds. For Pacific Northwest birders it is somewhat surprising that this species is one of the most abundant ducks in North America, because locally they only occur in very small numbers.

Cinnamon teal
Anas cyanoptera
Rare
Summer
Sites: Sportsman's and Egg Lakes, Roadside birding
Notes: While cinnamon teal occur all the way to the Pacific Coast in Oregon and California, in Washington they are uncommon west of the Cascades and are only rarely seen on San Juan Island. The Washington Breeding Bird Atlas does record evidence of cinnamon teal nesting in San Juan County between 1987 and 1996. An unusual case of an over-wintering bird was noted in 2000 (*WOS News* 67), but they are more likely to occur between April and September.

Northern shoveler
Anas clypeata
Common
Winter
Sites: False Bay, Sportsman's and Egg Lakes, Roadside birding
Notes: These ducks, with their distinctive large, flattened bills, prefer stagnant or muddy waters where they can sift through the floating vegetation for food. This type of freshwater habitat is scarce on the island, so shoveler only occur here in small numbers, with just a few dozen on the island during any given winter. They are known to breed in the Puget Sound region, but are unlikely to remain on the island in summer.

Northern shoveler

Northern pintail
Anas acuta
Abundant
Winter
Sites: False Bay, Sportsman's and Egg Lakes, Roadside birding
Notes: This species, often seen in large flocks of dozens to hundreds of birds, tends to hang out in different areas on the island from year to year depending on the marshes created by the level of seasonal flooding. Prime roadside places to look for them include just outside of Friday Harbor along Beaverton Valley Road and along Douglas and Bailer Hill Roads.

Green-winged teal
Anas crecca
Common
Winter
Sites: Jackson's Beach, Jakle's and Third Lagoons, False Bay
Notes: Rarely, green-winged teal may remain into the summer and breed here.

Canvasback
Aythya valisineria
Rare
Winter
Sites: False Bay, Sportsman's and Egg Lakes, Roadside birding
Notes: While about 2000 canvasback winter in western Washington, they tend to prefer marine bays and estuaries to the more open marine habitat found around San Juan Island. They are common in nearby Padilla, Skagit, and Samish Bays, but only occasionally seen here.

Ring-necked duck
Aythya collaris
Common
Winter
Sites: Jackson's Beach, Sportsman's and Egg Lakes, Roadside birding
Notes: Ring-necked ducks are more abundant in the winter, though a few remain to breed in the summer.

Lesser scaup

Greater scaup
Aythya marila
Rare
Winter
Sites: False Bay, English Camp, Sportsman's and Egg Lakes
Notes: The Salish Sea is one of the main winter destinations for this species along the Pacific Coast, but they tend to prefer marine bays and estuaries, a habitat not prevalent on San Juan Island. Christmas Bird Counts in the region have demonstrated a 50% decline in greater scaup since the mid-1970s, which makes them even more uncommon here than they used to be.

Lesser scaup
Aythya affinis
Uncommon
Winter
Sites: False Bay, English Camp, Sportsman's and Egg Lakes, Roadside birding
Notes: Lesser scaup are more likely to be seen on lakes and ponds than the very similar greater scaup, a species that prefers marine waters. Habitat is not enough to differentiate these species, however; head shape is the best clue. Additionally, if the lighting is right, the lesser scaup appears to have a purple sheen on the head, while the greater scaup looks green.

Harlequin duck
Histrionicus histrionicus
Common
Year-round
Sites: Jakle's and Third Lagoons, Cattle Point, The Westside
Notes: Harlequin ducks don't breed in the San Juan Islands (they move inland to fast moving streams to nest), but they are still found here year-round. They are probably most widespread in the winter when birds throughout the region feed coastally. When pairs head to their nesting grounds in the spring, sub-adult and non-breeding birds remain behind, sometimes in large flocks numbering up to a

hundred or more. As soon as the eggs are laid, the males return to the coast to molt while females stay behind and raise the chicks. Look for harlequin ducks perched on rocky outcroppings or camouflaged among kelp beds, rather than out in open water like the other sea ducks. Harlequin duck populations in the state have increased in recent decades.

Surf scoter
Melanitta perspicillata
Abundant
Winter
Sites: Fourth of July Beach, Cattle Point, South Beach
Notes: Scoters are bottom-feeders that primarily eat mollusks, which they swallow whole and grind up in their gizzards. In the winter, surf scoters are one of the most abundant sea ducks in local waters. Most depart by the end of May for their northern breeding grounds, but non-breeding immature scoters remain along the Pacific Coast during the summer instead. As a result, occasionally small numbers are seen in the San Juan Islands during the summer months as well.

White-winged scoter
Melanitta fusca
Uncommon
Winter
Sites: Fourth of July Beach, Cattle Point, South Beach
Notes: In areas where all three scoter species can be found (like San Juan Island), white-winged scoters tend to hang out in deeper waters further from shore than the other scoters. Griffin Bay is the best place to see them from shore on San Juan Island; they are often out in the middle of the bay mixed in with a larger flock of surf scoters. Numbers of over-wintering white-winged scoters vary widely from season to season. Sometimes flocks of several dozen can be regularly seen, while other years they are nearly absent.

Black scoter
Melanitta americana
Rare
Winter
Sites: Fourth of July Beach, Cattle Point, South Beach
Notes: While white-winged scoters and surf scoters are normally seen in flocks, black scoters seen near San Juan Island are usually solitary or in pairs, mixed in with other sea ducks.

Long-tailed duck
Clangula hyemalis
Uncommon
Winter
Sites: Jackson's Beach, Fourth of July Beach, South Beach
Notes: Formerly known as oldsquaw, the long-tailed duck is one of the most coveted species that birdwatchers come to San Juan Island to see. They can somewhat reliably be seen in the winter off South Beach where the offshore shelf makes for an ideal feeding site. They are seen less regularly in Griffin Bay, and are generally found in more open water and farther from shore than the scoters. They are often close enough to be seen through binoculars, but other times a scope is required to get a good look. While long-tailed ducks somewhat confusingly have three plumages instead of the traditional two, the long, central tail feathers that are the namesake for this species remain on the male year-round. The long tail often trails in the water and remains out of sight on sitting birds, but it is visible in flight as well as when the bird dives.

Bufflehead
Bucephala albeola
Abundant
Winter
Sites: Jackson's Beach, Fourth of July Beach, Roadside birding
Notes: The Salish Sea hosts some of the largest wintering concentrations of bufflehead, and hundreds can regularly be seen on San Juan Island from November-April. This species is one of the

few local sea birds that has not suffered a population decline, in part because of its more diverse diet that makes it more adaptable to change than other species. Look for them on almost all bodies of both fresh and salt water throughout the winter.

Common goldeneye
Bucephala clangula
Uncommon
Winter
Sites: Jackson's Beach, Jakle's and Third Lagoons, False Bay
Notes: This is the more likely goldeneye species to be encountered locally, with flocks of up to several dozen possible at Griffin Bay. The common goldeneye may be observed on either fresh or salt water, while the Barrow's goldeneye is almost exclusively seen on salt water.

Barrow's goldeneye
Bucephala islandica
Uncommon
Winter
Sites: Jackson's Beach, Jakle's and Third Lagoons, False Bay
Notes: Barrow's goldeneye occur in smaller numbers locally than common goldeneye, and in local waters pairs of this species are more likely to be encountered rather than larger flocks. Hybrids between the two species may also occur. 90% of the global population of this species resides on the Pacific Coast; the other 10% occurs in northeastern Canada.

Hooded merganser
Lophodytes cucullatus
Common
Year-round
Sites: Jackson's Beach, Westside Lake, Sportsman's and Egg Lakes, Roadside birding
Notes: The only merganser species regularly seen throughout the year, the hooded merganser is most abundant in the winter

when the local population is augmented by birds that breed in other areas. This species can be seen on small freshwater lakes year-round, generally avoiding the larger lakes that the common merganser inhabits. In the winter they are also seen along the marine coastline. In recent years pairs have nested at Westside Lake and the waters near Lakedale Resort on Roche Harbor Road.

Common merganser
Mergus merganser
Common
Winter
Sites: Roche Harbor Highlands (Briggs Lake), Sportsman's and Egg Lakes, Roadside birding
Notes: Common mergansers generally prefer large freshwater habitats, so they are most likely to be seen on some of the island's bigger lakes. Occasionally they are found on salt water as well, but in singles or small numbers. A few birds may breed here during some years, but they are far more common in the winter.

Red-breasted merganser
Mergus serrator
Common
Winter
Sites: Friday Harbor, South Beach, The Westside
Notes: Although all three merganser species can be seen in saltwater, the red-breasted merganser is the most likely to be seen in marine environments, the habitat they occupy exclusively during the winter months. You'll often see small groups diving in unison near the shoreline; they may be cooperatively herding a school of fish.

Ruddy duck
Oxyura jamaicensis
Occasional
Year-round
Sites: Roche Harbor Highlands (Briggs Lake), Sportsman and Egg Lakes, Roadside birding

Notes: Formerly common, the ruddy duck declined locally between the 1950s and 1970s and is now only occasionally seen. Like many other water birds, the reason for their decline is uncertain and probably multi-facted.

Very rare ducks
The Eurasian form of the green-winged teal, known as the **common teal**, is a regularly sighted accidental along the west coast of North America and thus an occasional visitor to the San Juan Islands. The common and green-winged teals have variably been considered races of the same species or separate species. Most international organizations currently recognize them as separate species, though the American Ornithological Union does not, so local records of this species are hard to come by. **Redheads** more commonly winter in eastern Washington or along the Columbia River at the southern border of the state. If seen on San Juan Island, they are likely passing through on migration, either in October-November or March-April. The **tufted duck**, a Eurasian species very similar to the ring-necked duck, is another unlikely visitor to the San Juan Islands, though it is seen periodically throughout the Pacific Northwest in winter. Look for one in with flocks of ring-necked ducks, greater scaup, or lesser scaup. There are two confirmed records of a **king eider** in San Juan County: one in February 1967 and one in October 1986 (Tweit and Skriletz 1996).

Pheasants and Quail

California quail
Callipepla californica
Common
Year-round
Sites: Cattle Point, American Camp, The Westside (Land Bank)
Notes: The California quail is one of many species that has been introduced to the island over the years (in this case as a game bird), but it is one of only a few that has thrived long-term. Since becoming established in the early 1900s, California quail are now year-round

breeding residents. Birds can be detected by their loud three-part call, though they can make a wide variety of vocalizations. Large family groups of a dozen or more birds are often seen in places like American Camp, Cattle Point, and while roadside birding. These groups of quail, called coveys, will stay together throughout the winter season before pairs split off to breed early in the following spring.

Ring-necked pheasant
Phasianus colchicus
Rare
Year-round
Sites: Friday Harbor, American Camp, English Camp
Notes: Ring-necked pheasants have been introduced to San Juan Island on multiple occasions but usually start to die out over time. As a result, the population fluctuates, with the species becoming more numerous after an introduction before eventually declining. In part due to rainfall coinciding with the hatching season, pheasant populations are generally not sustainable in western Washington. Pheasants were considered abundant on San Juan Island until the early 1970s before seemingly dying off completely. Small numbers were again reported starting in the mid-1990s, and declined again by the later 2000s. The author last saw one on the island in 2008. At least one was seen in 2011, but it was potentially a released captive bird.

Wild turkey
Meleagris gallopavo
Rare
Year-round
Sites: English Camp
Notes: Wild turkeys, like many other gallinaceous game birds, were introduced to the Islands in the mid-20th century, and were considered common and quite tame on San Juan Island through the 1990s. Since then, they have declined considerably and may have been extirpated from San Juan Island, though there is still a

population seen regularly on Lopez Island. Consider this species unlikely on San Juan unless it is reintroduced in the future.

Very rare gallinaceous birds
Ruffed grouse were historically reported in the islands in the early 20th century, but the only modern day report for this species was in August 2009 on Jones Island where they were heard twice and seen displaying once (Blake Hough, pers. comm.). Several other pheasant species were introduced to the San Juan Islands at various times for hunting purposes, but all have been locally extinct for more than 30 years (Lewis and Sharpe 1987). **Sooty grouse** are still occasionally reported in the higher elevation old growth forests of Orcas Island (Gayle Benton, pers. comm.).

Loons

Red-throated loon
Gavia stellata
Rare
Winter
Sites: Cattle Point, South Beach, American Camp
Notes: The slender red-throated loon used to be far more common in the Salish Sea, but the species has declined by as much as 70% since the 1970s. Numbers seen in inland waters vary from year to year.

Pacific loon
Gavia pacifica
Common
Winter
Sites: Cattle Point, South Beach, The Westside
Notes: The largest North American congregation of wintering Pacific loons occurs in the Salish Sea, with as many as 10,000 residing there. This is the only loon species regularly encountered in large flocks. From the 1970s-1990s, groups of several hundred loons were regularly seen, though groups on the order of one or

two dozen are more the norm now. When Pacific loons arrive in the fall, and before they depart in the spring (they are usually seen through May), they may be seen in breeding plumage.

Common loon
Gavia immer
Common
Winter
Sites: Fourth of July Beach, Cattle Point, American Camp, South Beach
Notes: While common loons breed on freshwater lakes, they are seen almost exclusively on saltwater locally. They are far more common in the winter, but a few non-breeders stay around during the summer. These residents as well as some migrants may be seen in summer plumage. Occasionally they are even heard giving their eerie call, one commonly associated with the sound of the wilderness.

Very rare loons
In 1985, the Pacific loon and **Arctic loon** were split and became separate species. There have only been a handful of Arctic loon records in Washington since then. While none of these have been in San Juan County, it should be considered a hypothetical species. **The yellow-billed loon** is a species seen annually in small numbers in the Strait of Juan de Fuca in winter months, but seldom do they come as far inland as the San Juan Islands. The most likely place to encounter one is off of South Beach or Cattle Point.

Grebes

Pied-billed grebe
Podilymbus podiceps
Uncommon
Year-round
Sites: Sportsman's and Egg Lakes, Westside Lake, roadside ponds

Notes: Unlike other grebes, pied-billeds spend the entire year on freshwater lakes and ponds, though during freezing spells they may be forced to retreat to marine habitats. In an interesting adaptation for a diving bird, they can actually "submarine", or descend straight down into the water. Sometimes you will just see their heads poking out from underwater.

Horned grebe
Podiceps auritus
Common
Winter
Sites: Fourth of July Beach, Cattle Point, South Beach
Notes: Horned grebes are the most numerous grebe species seen in the San Juan Islands. When they arrive in the fall they are generally already in their black-and-white winter plumage, but by April they molt into their black and red breeding plumage, complete with the feathered yellow horns that give them their name. They can be seen in the Islands until early May.

Red-necked grebe
Podiceps grisegena
Common
Winter
Sites: Fourth of July Beach, Cattle Point, South Beach
Notes: One of the most concentrated populations of wintering red-necked grebes occurs in the Salish Sea, where the species is one of three or four grebes that can be expected on any given day. They are more likely to be seen hanging out with surf scoters rather than with horned grebes.

Eared grebe
Podiceps nigricollis
Rare
Migration
Sites: Fourth of July Beach, Cattle Point, South Beach

Notes: The majority of the eared grebe population winters off the California coast, with only a small part of the population scattering over the rest of the west coast. It is most likely to be seen during migration.

Western grebe
Aechmophorus occidentalis
Uncommon
Winter
Sites: Cattle Point, South Beach, American Camp
Notes: Many Salish Sea marine bird species have experienced regional population declines, but none may be as dramatic as that of the western grebe which has decreased by as much as 95% since the 1970s. Considered an indicator species in ecosystems in which it occurs, factors that play a role in its decline include industrial contaminants, oil spills, degradation of lake and marsh habitat where they breed, and increased human disturbance from motor boat use. Sadly, today it's hard to imagine the flocks of thousands of western grebes that used to be seen in local waters.

Clark's grebe
Aechmophorus clarkii
Occasional
Winter
Sites: Cattle Point, South Beach, American Camp
Notes: Split from the western grebe in 1983, there are only a handful of county records for this species. It may go under-reported due to its similarity to the western grebe. When it does occur, it is usually just a single bird.

Tubenoses

Sooty shearwater
Puffinus griseus
Occasional
Summer
Sites: Cattle Point, South Beach
Notes: During some years shearwaters come to inland waters via the Strait of Juan de Fuca, and they may be visible from shore looking out towards the major straits. These influxes are most likely to happen during the shearwaters' southbound migration along the outer coast of Washington in the fall around September, and seem to vary from year to year depending on oceanic conditions and potentially El Niño/La Niña events. They are also more likely to head inland after a storm.

Very rare tubenoses
The sooty shearwater is the most likely pelagic species to be seen this far inland, but other pelagic species may be seen after heavy winds or during an especially large invasion year into the Strait of Juan de Fuca. **Black-footed albatrosses** are regularly recorded in the Strait of Juan de Fuca as well and it wouldn't be surprising for one to eventually occur in San Juan County, though they are currently only a hypothetical visitor. The best place to look for all of these species is in the Strait of Juan de Fuca from areas like South Beach and, even less likely, in Haro Strait. **Northern fulmars** are on record, though there haven't been any published sightings in the county since 1985 (Lewis and Sharpe 1987). The author recorded the first San Juan County record for the **pink-footed shearwater** in September 2009 during a large sooty shearwater invasion. **Short-tailed shearwaters**, and, increasingly, **Manx shearwaters**, are seen in the Strait of Juan de Fuca and have both been reported in the county. Manx shearwaters have most recently been seen in June 2004 near the Matia Island group (*WOS News* 96). There is only a single county record for the **short-tailed shearwater** in December of 1977 (Lewis and Sharpe

1977). **Fork-tailed storm-petrels** have been seen on numerous occasions. A single storm-petrel was photographed in Cattle Pass in May 2011 (Nan Simpson, pers. comm.) and several more were seen on following days (Katie Jones, pers. comm.). This is the first published record of this species in the county since the mid-1980s. There is also a single account of a **Leach's storm-petrel** in Rosario Strait in October 1981 (Lewis and Sharpe 1987).

Cormorants

Brandt's cormorant
Phalacrocorax penicillatus
Uncommon
Year-round
Sites: Cattle Point, South Beach, The Westside
Notes: Once common, the Brandt's cormorant has declined locally and no longer breeds here, perhaps because of increased human shoreline activity during the summer. Flocks from Oregon and California migrate northward after breeding and can be seen in the San Juan Islands starting in late summer; it is unknown whether the birds from the few Washington outer-coast breeding sites also roam inland during the non-breeding season. In the winter months one of the best locations to see Brandt's cormorants is in Cattle Pass, where the strong tidal currents fit their preferred foraging habitat. They regularly roost near here at sites like Goose Island and Whale Rocks. Occasionally exceptionally large groups of several hundred birds are reported. A few non-breeding birds may remain in the islands throughout the summer, but in smaller numbers than they used to, and they are generally considered rare this time of year.

Double-crested cormorant
Phalacrocorax auritus
Abundant
Year-round
Sites: Cattle Point, English Camp, Sportsman's Lake

Double-crested cormorant

Notes: Double-crested cormorants have increased in numbers in recent decades and are the only cormorant species to be seen in freshwater as well as saltwater habitats. They nest on flat sites where they build tall stick nests in places such as Goose Island near Cattle Point. Many roost on coastal islands, but others roost in trees. Tree roosting regularly occurs just outside of Friday Harbor as well as at Sportsman's Lake. The kinked neck of the double-crested cormorant helps distinguish it from other cormorants in flight.

Pelagic cormorant
Phalacrocorax pelagicus
Abundant
Year-round
Sites: Cattle Point, South Beach, The Westside
Notes: Pelagic cormorants have also experienced a population increase in recent decades. They are cliff nesters, and have several nesting sites within San Juan County, however they show little site fidelity and change breeding locations every few years. The white-stained rocks on many cliffs show the remnants of a former pelagic cormorant colony.

Very rare Suliformes
In the summer of 2005, a **brown booby** was recorded on multiple occasions near Bellingham, Washington and in August of that year

presumably the same bird was seen off the south end of San Juan Island (*WOS News* 103). This was the first San Juan County record for this species, however in 1997 a brown booby was seen near Port Townsend, so they should be considered an accidental visitor to the Salish Sea.

Pelicans

American white pelican
Pelecanus erythrorhynchos
Occasional
Winter
Sites: Sportsman's and Egg Lakes, Roadside birding
Notes: While not an expected species, white pelicans roam sporadically in small numbers, particularly in the fall. They could end up on San Juan Island just as easily as anywhere else in western Washington, and there were reports in the county in 2005, August 2007 (*WOS News* 115), and 2008.

Brown pelican
Pelecanus occidentalis
Rare
Summer
Sites: Cattle Point, South Beach, American Camp
Notes: The brown pelican was removed from the Endangered Species List in 2009 after the population recovered from DDT-related threats. Brown pelicans typically wander north from their breeding grounds in late summer, and most local records occur in August and September. In recent years their range has been expanding northward steadily. As a result, this species may become more common in the region.

Herons

Great blue heron
Ardea herodias
Common
Year-round
Sites: Jackson's Beach, Jakle's and Third Lagoons, False Bay
Notes: Throughout most of its range, great blue herons are associated with freshwater marshes, but on San Juan Island they are most commonly seen along the marine coastline. The most reliable places to look for great blue herons are in the tidal flats of False Bay, in lagoons, or perched on kelp beds, particularly along the west side of San Juan Island.

Great blue heron

Great egret
Ardea alba
Occasional
Year-round
Sites: Jackson's Beach, Jakle's and Third Lagoons, The Westside
Notes: Great egrets were nearly extirpated in the late 19th century after being hunted for their ornamental feathers. After receiving

protection in the early 20th century, they rapidly recovered, and expanded into Washington in the late 1970s. While more commonly found in the southern part of the state, some do stray further north, particularly in late summer after breeding. One was seen near Lime Kiln Lighthouse in June 2011 (Mark Lewis, pers. comm.), and there were sightings on Lopez Island in May 2006 (*WOS News* 107) and September 2000 (*WOS News* 73).

Green heron
Butorides virescens
Occasional
Summer
Sites: False Bay Drive (Panorama Marsh), Roadside birding
Notes: Only reported a handful of times historically, sightings of this species have become more frequent in recent years. Though still unlikely, it should now be considered a possibility. Some of the smaller roadside ponds are probably the most likely place to detect one when they do show up.

Very rare herons
Over the years there have been reports of **American bitterns**, including several possible accounts over the last decade, though none have been confirmable. A single **black-crowned night heron** was reported in the winter of 1976-77 on Orcas Island (Lewis and Sharpe 1987).

Raptors

Turkey Vulture
Cathartes aura
Common
Summer
Sites: False Bay and False Bay Drive, Mt. Young and Mitchell Hill, Roadside Birding
Notes: Turkey vultures are expected on San Juan Island from March through September. These carrion-feeders are often seen cruising

over the farmlands in the inland parts of the island, with multiple birds congregating when a carcass has been located. Large groups can also be seen as they gather preceding the fall migration. It is not unheard of for a few vultures to remain over the winter. Birds have been recorded during every Christmas Bird Count since 2004, usually on Lopez Island.

Osprey
Pandion haliaetus
Uncommon
Summer
Sites: Friday Harbor, English Camp
Notes: A lot of prime habitat for osprey exists in the San Juan Islands, but they occur in smaller numbers here than may be expected, probably due in part to competition with the larger bald eagle which is known for stealing fish from osprey. There are multiple nests on San Juan Island as well as on surrounding islands, and breeding pairs will defend these territories fiercely from eagles. The most visible nest is at English Camp. It was first constructed

Osprey

in 1996 and has been rebuilt on a couple of occasions after being blown down by high winds over the winter. There is another osprey nest just outside of Friday Harbor and the birds from this nest are regularly seen flying over the harbor.

Bald eagle
Haliaeetus leucocephalus
Common
Year-round
Sites: Cattle Point, American Camp, Roadside birding
Notes: The bald eagle is only scarce during a period from late August to early October when many birds go to nearby mainland rivers to feed on salmon runs. The rest of the year they are common, as the San Juan Islands have one of the densest breeding populations of bald eagles in the Lower 48.

Bald eagles

Northern harrier
Circus cyaneus
Uncommon
Winter
Sites: Cattle Point, South Beach, American Camp
Notes: Distinctive with their long tails and white rumps, northern harriers hunt by gliding over prairies like those at the south end of the island. This species is sexually dimorphic, with males being gray while females and juveniles are brown. Northern harriers are most common during the winter, with migrating birds also occurring during the spring and fall. Interestingly, this hawk is usually absent in the summer, though it is commonly found on the Washington mainland year-round and is known to breed on nearby Whidbey Island.

Sharp-shinned hawk
Accipiter striatus
Uncommon
Year-round
Sites: Friday Harbor, Roadside birding
Notes: While there are year-round reports of sharp-shinned hawks on San Juan Island, they tend to breed at higher elevations and thus are primarily here in the winter. They should also be expected in greater numbers during migration (April and September-October). Their similarity to the Cooper's hawk makes identification confusing and abundance reports unreliable. These hawks loiter where their songbird prey is common, including near bird feeders.

Cooper's hawk
Accipiter cooperii
Uncommon
Year-round
Sites: Mt. Finlayson, Roadside birding
Notes: While in most lowlands in western Washington the Cooper's hawk is outnumbered by the sharp-shinned hawk in the winter, they generally occur in about equal numbers on San Juan Island.

Distinguishing the two species in the field can be difficult, however, and reports can be unreliable.

Red-tailed hawk
Buteo jamaicensis
Common
Year-round
Sites: Mt. Finlayson, The Westside (Land Bank) Roadside birding
Notes: Red-tailed hawks have a diverse diet, which has helped them adapt to a wide variety of habitats. As a result, this resident breeder can be seen throughout the island, but it is especially fun to watch them on Mt. Finlayson, where along with other raptors they cruise in the updrafts created by marine winds hitting the hillside. More hawks are here in the winter when the resident population is supplemented by birds from further north and inland. The wide variety of color morphs can make this hawk difficult to identify, but it is the most common hawk on the island.

Red-tailed hawk

Rough-legged hawk
Buteo lagopus
Rare
Winter
Sites: Mt. Finlayson, Roadside birding
Notes: An erratic winter visitor, this Arctic hawk occurs in low numbers throughout Washington and may be more common on the island in some years and completely absent in others. There are no clear trends to its cyclical occurrence.

Golden eagle
Aquila chrysaetos
Rare
Year-round
Sites: Mt. Finlayson, American Camp
Notes: Many people mistake immature bald eagles for golden eagles, a species that nested on San Juan Island until at least 1988 but is now only rarely seen here. Requiring large territories, golden eagles probably ceased to breed on the island as more development occurred. A decline in rabbits, one of their prey items, probably also played a role. Goldens are now more likely to be seen on Orcas Island than on San Juan Island, where a pair may still nest on Turtleback Mountain. Immature migrating birds are the most likely to be encountered.

American kestrel
Falco sparverius
Rare
Year-round
Sites: American Camp, False Bay and False Bay Drive, Roadside birding
Notes: Like many of our other raptors, this species is more likely seen during migration. Kestrels used to breed here, but sightings have decreased in recent years. Spring migration peaks in western Washington during April and May, while fall migration occurs primarily during September and October.

Merlin
Falco columbarius
Uncommon
Year-round
Sites: Cattle Point, False Bay and False Bay Drive, Roadside birding
Notes: More common than its cousin the kestrel, local merlins feed on shorebirds in addition to small passerines and so are often found near sites like False Bay and Cattle Point.

Peregrine falcon
Falco peregrinus
Uncommon
Year-round
Sites: Cattle Point, The Westside (Lime Kiln Point State Park), False Bay
Notes: Peregrine falcons prefer to build their nests on ledges of steep rocky cliffs near water. The state's densest breeding population occurs throughout the San Juan Islands, where some pairs occupy their territories year-round. Cold temperatures and heavy rain have been associated with local nesting failure, including in 1996 and 2000 (Hayes and Buchanan 2002). While falcons on the outer coast are more likely to take auklets and murres, some of the most common prey species for peregrines in the San Juans are starlings, robins, and rock pigeons. The peregrine falcon experienced dramatic declines starting in the 1950s from extensive pesticide use that caused nesting failure due to thin egg shells, and in the 1970s there was only one confirmed nesting site in Washington. After DDT was banned in the early 1970s, and helped by the release of captive-born birds from 1982-1997, peregrine falcons have made a substantial recovery in the state and throughout the nation. The peregrine falcon was removed from the Endangered Species List in the United States in 1999. While there are reports of the Peale's subspecies occurring in the San Juan Islands, it is now generally accepted that it is the American subspecies found here.

Very rare raptors

There are multiple confirmed sightings of the **gyrfalcon** in San Juan County. One was recorded during the 1993 Christmas Bird Count, though a bird seen in January 1994 on San Juan Island had falconer's jesses (*WOS News* 31), and others have likely been escaped birds as well. The most recent one was reported in December 2004 at Sucia Island (*eBird*). **Northern goshawks** also occur periodically, with the most recent confirmed sighting being in 2007 (Gayle Benton, pers. comm.). The following raptor species have been reported five or fewer times in San Juan County (with most recent published sighting in parenthesis): **Swainson's hawk** (June 1997, *eBird*), **ferruginous hawk** (unconfirmed 1970, Lewis and Sharpe 1987), and **prairie falcon** (1973, Lewis and Sharpe 1987).

Rails and Cranes

Virginia rail
Rallus limicola
Uncommon
Year-round
Sites: False Bay Drive (Panorama Marsh), Roadside birding
Notes: Rarely seen, these rails are most easily detected by their "kiddick-kiddick-kiddick" call heard mostly in the spring.

Sora
Porzana carolina
Uncommon
Summer
Sites: False Bay Drive (Panorama Marsh), Sportsman's and Egg Lakes, Roadside birding
Notes: Like the Virginia rail, the sora is very elusive and most likely to be detected by its loud descending call in the spring. April and May are the best months to hear it. One of the only places this species is regularly detected is at Panorama Marsh along False Bay

Drive. It has also been heard at the Swan Valley wetlands along San Juan Valley Road.

American coot
Fulica americana
Uncommon
Year-round
Sites: False Bay Drive (Panorama Marsh), Sportsman's and Egg Lakes, Roadside birding
Notes: An uncommon sighting at any time of year, the coot is slightly more abundant during the winter, while only a few birds may remain to breed.

Very rare cranes
Sandhill cranes are infrequently seen or heard flying overhead and have been reported stopping over on San Juan Island a couple of times during their southbound migration between August and October. There are reports of single birds stopping over for less than a day in the autumn of both 2004 and 2009 (Debby Clausen, pers. comm.), and two birds were seem on San Juan Island in September 2000 (*WOS News* 73).

Shorebirds

Black-bellied plover
Pluvialis squatarola
Uncommon
Winter
Sites: Fourth of July Beach, South Beach, False Bay
Notes: Small numbers of black-bellied plovers spend the winter here but greater numbers are seen during migration in April-May and September-October. Birds at the beginning or end of migration may be seen in summer plumage, but primarily winter plumage birds are seen. Look for the distinct black "arm-pits" that differentiate them from other similar plovers, though these other species should be considered very unlikely locally.

Black-bellied plovers

Semipalmated plover
Charadrius semipalmatus
Rare
Migration
Sites: Fourth of July Beach, Jakle's Lagoon, South Beach, False Bay
Notes: This migrant is usually detected heading north in April-May, and heading south in August-September. Individuals are likely to visit the same stopover sites from year to year, so it's just a matter of timing it right to see this species on San Juan Island.

Killdeer
Charadrius vociferus
Uncommon
Year-round
Sites: Jackson's Beach, Jakle's and Third Lagoons, False Bay
Notes: The most widespread American plover, killdeer are more abundant on San Juan Island during migration and winter. During this time of year groups of a dozen or more birds can be found, particularly on the gravel spit at Jackson's Beach

Black oystercatcher
Haematopus bachmani
Common
Year-round
Sites: Cattle Point, The Westside, San Juan County Park
Notes: Black oystercatchers are non-migrating shorebirds that can easily camouflage against the rocks, but become conspicuous when giving their loud, whistling call, especially when in flight. More common in the San Juan Islands than in Puget Sound to the south, the black oystercatcher is considered a keystone species indicating the health of rocky intertidal habitats along the North Pacific coast since they are relatively sensitive to disturbance. About 400 of the global population of 10,000 black oystercathcers live in Washington, and there are numerous nesting sites throughout the San Juans, including Low Island just offshore of San Juan County Park. Family groups of birds often remain together until the next breeding season, and during this time juvenile birds learn various foraging techniques from their parents. Large flocks of several dozen non-breeding birds are occasionally seen throughout the winter.

Black oystercatcher

Spotted sandpiper
Acititis macularius
Rare
Migration
Sites: False Bay, Jakle's Lagoon
Notes: As the most widespread sandpiper in North America, spotted sandpipers can be found near any type of water. Locally, they are more often seen on remote coasts of smaller islands rather than on San Juan Island itself. It's unlikely they breed here, so look for them during migration in May and September.

Wandering tattler
Tringa incana
Occasional
Migration
Sites: Cattle Point, The Westside, San Juan County Park
Notes: The rocky shoreline habitat preferred by wandering tattlers is common around San Juan Island, but in general the species prefers the outer coast of Washington over inland waters. When the birds are in the Salish Sea, they are more often seen on remote coasts of smaller rocky islands rather than on San Juan Island itself. Some of the best places to look for this species from shore include Goose Island near Cattle Point and Low Island near San Juan County Park. May is the peak of the northbound migration, while southbound birds may be encountered from July into September.

Greater yellowlegs
Tringa melanoleuca
Uncommon
Winter
Sites: Jackson's Beach, Jakle's and Third Lagoons, False Bay
Notes: When migrating through, greater yellowlegs may occur at any one of several locations, but the best place to look for this species in the winter is at Argyle Lagoon at Jackson's Beach where it is one of the most regularly occurring shorebirds. Usually at least one or two over-winter at that location.

Lesser yellowlegs
Tringa flavipes
Rare
Migration
Sites: Jackson's Beach, Jakle's Lagoon, False Bay
Notes: Rarer on San Juan Island than its larger cousin the greater yellowlegs, the lesser can be distinguished by its shorter bill and shorter vocalizations in flight (usually one to three notes, rather than three or more as given by the greater). This species will pass through during migration, typically April-May in the spring and August-September in the fall. It is unlikely to spend the winter here.

Whimbrel
Numenius phaeopus
Rare
Migration
Sites: South Beach, False Bay and False Bay Drive, Roadside birding
Notes: Like many of the less common shorebirds on San Juan Island, the whimbrel is a rare sight during migration, often only seen as a flyover. Sightings are most likely to occur in April-May and August-September. Unlike many of our other shorebirds, it may stop over on farm fields in addition to the coastline.

Ruddy turnstone
Arenaria interpres
Occasional
Migration
Sites: Jackson's Beach, Cattle Point, American Camp
Notes: Look for the occasional migrating ruddy turnstone in mixed flocks of other shorebirds, particularly black turnstones on San Juan Island. Peak sightings in the state occur in May and again in July and August.

Black turnstone
Arenaria melanocephala
Uncommon
Winter
Sites: Jackson's Beach, Cattle Point, American Camp
Notes: This species is more common on some of the more remote islands but can be seen in smaller numbers on San Juan Island in appropriate habitats. Flocks can easily be camouflaged against the rocks, but a careful search can usually turn up a few of these winter residents, particularly on the rocks off Cattle Point and in Grandma's Cove at American Camp. When they take flight they become suddenly conspicuous with their bold black-and-white wing markings.

Black turnstone

Surfbird
Aphriza virgata
Uncommon
Winter
Sites: Cattle Point, South Beach, American Camp

Notes: Surfbirds tend to prefer the outer coast of Washington over inland waters, but sometimes they are seen mixed in with local flocks of black turnstones.

Sanderling
Calidris alba
Uncommon
Migration
Sites: Fourth of July Beach, South Beach, False Bay
Notes: There is not a lot of the sandy habitat that these birds prefer on San Juan Island. When they stop over during migration, they settle for the gravelly beaches at places like South Beach and along Griffin Bay. The spring migration occurs mostly in April and May, and the fall migration starts as early as July. Sometimes birds are also encountered during the winter months.

Dunlin
Calidris alpina
Uncommon
Winter
Sites: Cattle Point, False Bay
Notes: About 90% of Washington's over-wintering shorebirds are dunlin, and they are found in great numbers at Padilla, Samish, and Skagit Bays on the mainland. They are less numerous on San Juan Island, and are usually reported during the Christmas Bird Counts in numbers ranging from a few dozen to 100-200.

Semipalmated sandpiper
Calidris pusilla
Occasional
Migration
Sites: Fourth of July Beach, South Beach, False Bay
Notes: This Calidris sandpiper is especially similar to the western sandpiper, and differentiation in the field can be difficult as both have black legs and similar coloration. The semipalmated is overall more petite than the western with a shorter, straighter bill and

lighter streaking below. The migratory routes of this species seem to vary from year to year, and in general it is more likely to be encountered during the fall migration (July-August) than during the spring (May). Your best chances of finding a semipalmated sandpiper are mixed in with large flocks of other peeps.

Western sandpiper
Calidris mauri
Uncommon
Migration
Sites: Fourth of July Beach, South Beach, False Bay
Notes: Western sandpipers are the most abundant shorebird in Washington, and thus it is no surprise that they are also the most commonly encountered species on San Juan Island. While they neither breed nor overwinter here, several million birds migrate through the state and stopovers to refuel are a crucial part of their journey. Locally, western sandpipers feed primarily on amphipods, so they are found at appropriate beach sites that have their preferred prey available. Distinguish westerns from the other peeps by their black legs, chestnut patch on their scapular "shoulder" feathers, and behavior of readily wading into the water. Fall migration begins in July and continues through September, while spring migration is concentrated in April and May.

Least sandpiper

Least sandpiper
Calidris minutilla
Uncommon
Migration
Sites: Fourth of July Beach, South Beach, False Bay
Notes: Similar to the other small sandpipers known as "peeps" and migrating at the exact same time as western sandpipers, least sandpipers have pale yellowish legs and prefer to stay out of the water, which can help to distinguish them in the field.

Short-billed dowitcher
Limnodromus griseus
Rare
Migration
Sites: Jackson's Beach, False Bay
Notes: Short-billed and long-billed dowitchers were considered the same species until 1950, and are best distinguished by call. Both are more commonly seen throughout other parts of western Washington than in the San Juan Islands, but look for them during the peak of their migratory periods in April-May and July-September.

Long-billed dowitcher
Limnodromus scolopaceus
Rare
Migration
Sites: Jackson's Beach, False Bay
Notes: Also a rare visitor, the long-billed dowitcher is more likely to be seen on San Juan Island than the very similar short-billed.

Wilson's snipe
Gallinago delicata
Uncommon
Year-round
Sites: False Bay and False Bay Drive, Roadside birding
Notes: These secretive birds are more numerous during migration,

but are most easily detected by their spring winnowing during aerial displays put on by resident breeders. Look and listen for them particularly at dusk and dawn in open habitats, usually marshes. Migrating birds peak in March and from August-October.

Wilson's phalarope
Phalaropus tricolor
Occasional
Migration
Sites: Jakle's and Third Lagoons, Roadside birding
Notes: Unlike the other phalarope species, Wilson's phalaropes tend to avoid marine waters during migration. Look for this rare visitor to western Washington during May and June, primarily on lagoons and ponds.

Red-necked phalarope
Phalaropus lobatus
Uncommon
Migration
Sites: Cattle Point, American Camp, The Westside
Notes: This species readily changes its migratory path depending on oceanic currents and winds, so the numbers seen from year to year can vary widely. Smaller northbound flocks in the spring (mostly May) are a rarer sight than the more dependable large flocks, numbering up to several hundred birds, seen in Haro Strait and Cattle Pass every August and September.

Red phalarope
Phalaropus fulicarius
Occasional
Migration
Sites: Cattle Point, South Beach, The Westside
Notes: Red phalaropes migrate well offshore, but are intermittently pushed towards land during heavy wind storms. Peak sightings occur in the Strait of Juan de Fuca in May and October, though every few winters they are reported in greater numbers. There

have been a handful of sightings in San Juan County, including in August 2000 (*WOS News* 73), but they are almost exclusively from boats. A shore-based sighting of two birds occurred from Cattle Point in December 1998 (*WOS News* 61).

Very rare shorebirds
Many other shorebird species are known to migrate along the Washington coast and very occasionally may show up in inland waters. There have been reports in San Juan County of the following species (most recent published county sighting in parentheses, with source): **American and Pacific golden plovers** (April 2000 at American Camp, *WOS News* 70), **black-necked stilt** (August 1977 at Cattle Point, Lewis and Sharpe 1987), **American avocet** (June 1999 at American Camp, *WOS News* 64), **solitary sandpiper** (unknown date, Lewis and Sharpe 1987), **willet** (July 2006, *eBird*), **long-billed curlew** (May 2005 at American Camp, *WOS News* 101), **marbled godwit** (April 2011 at False Bay, sighted by the author), **red knot** (Lopez Island 2008, Gayle Benton pers.comm.; and July 2004, *WOS News* 96), **Baird's sandpiper** (September 2010 at False Bay, Blake Hough, pers. comm.), **pectoral sandpiper** (August 2010 at Fourth of July Beach, *eBird*), **sharp-tailed sandpiper** (October 1996 on Lopez Island, *WOS News* 50), **rock sandpiper** (April 2002 on Sucia Island, *eBird*), **stilt sandpiper** (October 2008 with a flock of western sandpipers on Henry Island, Blake Hough, pers. comm.), and **buff-breasted sandpiper** (September 1979 at American Camp, Lewis and Sharpe 1987).

Gulls

Black-legged kittiwake
Rissa tridactyla
Occasional
Year-round
Sites: Cattle Point, South Beach, The Westside
Notes: Like other pelagic species, kittiwakes are more expected in the Strait of Juan de Fuca than in inland waters, though there

have been multiple reports of this species around San Juan Island over the years. Sightings have occurred all throughout the year, but are most likely in the fall and early winter, particularly after heavy wind storms.

Sabine's gull
Xema sabini
Occasional
Summer
Sites: Cattle Point
Notes: Generally considered a more pelagic gull species, Sabine's gulls are periodically sighted in inland waters, usually between May and October. While more sightings occur in the Strait of Juan de Fuca, they have also been seen in Rosario and Haro Straits.

Bonaparte's gull
Chroicocephalus philadelphia
Uncommon
Migration
Sites: Cattle Point, The Westside, Reuben Tarte County Park
Notes: Bonaparte's gulls breed in the northern taiga forests of Canada, and pass through the San Juan Islands on both their spring (February-May) and fall (August-November) migrations. The distinct black hoods are most likely to be seen on early spring migrants; the rest of the time they are in their non-breeding plumage. Bonaparte's gulls often congregate in large flocks to feed where turbulent currents come together, including in Boundary Pass and Spieden Channel. Unfortunately neither of these areas are easily visible from any public lands on San Juan Island. While large flocks can also be seen from the Anacortes ferry, particularly in Rosario Strait, the best place to look for them from the shores of San Juan Island is to the north of Reuben Tarte County Park and off of Lime Kiln Point State Park. Individual birds may be seen anywhere along the coast, particularly in April-May and September-October. Historically they were regularly seen at False Bay.

Bonaparte's gull (breeding plumage)

Heermann's gull
Lanus heermanni
Abundant
Summer
Sites: Cattle Point, American Camp, The Westside
Notes: Heermann's gulls have unusual movement patterns: they breed south of the US off the coast of Mexico, then after breeding concludes in July they head north along the Pacific coast as far as British Columbia to feed. Locally they occur in large numbers from mid-July through October, when they begin to head back south to their breeding grounds. Look for them roosting in large flocks along rocky shorelines, particularly off the southwest end of the island.

Mew gull
Larus canus
Abundant
Winter
Sites: Friday Harbor, Jackson's Beach, False Bay
Notes: Large flocks of this species can reliably be found at False Bay, where during the right tidal conditions they will foot-paddle in the mud for food.

Mew gull

Ring-billed gull
Larus delawarensis
Rare
Year-round
Sites: Friday Harbor, False Bay, South Beach
Notes: Winter flocks of ring-billed gulls are common throughout Puget Sound, but are less often seen further north here in the San Juan Islands. This gull also tends to be more common inland rather than along the coasts. Non-breeding birds may remain in the Salish Sea throughout the summer, so small numbers of this species may be encountered any time of year.

Western gull
Larus occidentalis
Uncommon
Year-round
Sites: Cattle Point, South Beach, False Bay
Notes: The Salish Sea is in the northernmost part of the western gull's range, and throughout the region it commonly hybridizes with the glaucous-winged gull forming what some refer to as an Olympic gull. In general, northern western gulls have a paler

mantle than those seen further to the south, so distinguishing purebreds from hybrids, especially when factoring in backcrosses, can be difficult in the field.

California gull
Larus californicus
Uncommon
Migration
Sites: South Beach, American Camp, False Bay
Notes: Locally, California gulls undergo more of an east-west migration, breeding in inland Washington and wintering along the outer coast of the state. Peak numbers occur around San Juan Island during the late summer and throughout the fall, but most of these birds eventually continue on to the outer coast for the rest of the winter rather than staying in the Salish Sea. A few non-breeders may also be seen during the summer months.

Herring gull
Larus argentatus
Rare
Winter
Sites: Jackson's Beach, South Beach, False Bay
Notes: Herring gulls breed in British Columbia, and as soon as the nesting season has concluded birds disperse. They primarily head for the outer coast of Washington, but they may be seen in the Salish Sea. Look for them mixed in with flocks of other gull species, especially in bait ball congregations out in the straits.

Thayer's gull
Larus thayeri
Uncommon
Winter
Sites: South Beach, False Bay
Notes: Formerly considered a sub-species of the herring gull, and now considered by some a subspecies of the Iceland gull, the Thayer's gull is easily confused with many other local gull species

and hybrids and probably goes well under-reported. It is especially similar to the glaucous-winged x western gull hybrid that is common here. In flocks of large gulls, look for the deeper pink leg color of a Thayer's to help pick one out of the crowd.

Glaucous-winged gull
Larus glaucescens
Abundant
Year-round
Sites: Cattle Point, False Bay, The Westside
Notes: Over the last few decades, glaucous-winged gulls have experienced a range expansion and population increase. Some of the densest summer concentrations of glaucous-winged gulls occur in the Salish Sea, where it is by far the most common gull seen on San Juan Island. Hybrids with western gulls, sometimes referred to as Olympic gulls, are regularly seen.

Glaucous-winged gull

Very rare gulls

A single record of a **black-headed gull** occurred in September 1987 (Tweit and Paulson 1994). **Little gulls** and **Franklin's gulls** (August 2003 near Lopez Island, *WOS News* 91) can be seen in with large flocks of Bonaparte's gulls on occasion. The Alaskan **glaucous gull** occasionally ventures south to the Lower 48 in winter, though it seems to occur less often in the Salish Sea region than elsewhere in the Pacific Northwest; usually it is immatures that wander this far.

Terns and Jaegers

Caspian tern
Hydroprogne caspia
Uncommon
Summer
Sites: Jackson's Beach, South Beach, False Bay
Notes: Caspian tern numbers have increased substantially in the Pacific Northwest since the mid-1980s, with some local populations doubling or even tripling. There is a Caspian tern nesting colony on March Point near Anacortes, and there was another large nesting colony on Dungeness Spit on the Olympic Peninsula. Starting in 2009, a new colony formed along the Bellingham waterfront on the property of an abandoned paper mill and many of the Dungeness Spit birds moved to this new location. In 2010 an estimated 3000 birds nested there, mostly abandoning the former breeding location. In early 2011, the future of this new Bellingham colony was in jeopardy as Port of Bellingham officials planned to deter the terns from returning so they could conduct environmental clean-up work near the site without having to avoid the protected terns. As a result, they may end up relocating their nesting colony again. Under normal conditions, it's not unusual for Caspian terns to move to a new breeding colony site every few years.

Common tern
Sterna hirundo
Occasional
Migration
Sites: Jackson's Beach, South Beach, False Bay
Notes: The nearest breeding colonies for this species are in Alberta and Montana, and after that the young fledged birds disperse for a short time period before migrating south. Look for them near San Juan Island from August into early November. They tend not to pass through on their way back to their breeding grounds in May and June. This species used to be far more common in the San Juan Islands than it is today, but the birds now tend to go elsewhere, probably due to declines in herring and bait fish.

Parasitic jaeger
Stercorarius parasiticus
Occasional
Migration
Sites: Cattle Point, South Beach
Notes: The parasitic jaeger is the most common jaeger species to be seen this far inland. As common terns have declined in inland waters so have the parasitic jaegers, which as kleptoparasites harass smaller birds to drop their prey. They may still be seen pestering some of the smaller gulls like the Heermann's and Bonaparte's, so keep an eye out for them near large flocks of these species. The best chance to see them is in May or August-October.

Very rare terns and jaegers
Black terns are expected in the eastern part of the state but only rarely wander west of the Cascades. There have been no confirmed sightings since the three reported in the 1980s in Lewis and Sharpe (1987). From 1977 to 1995, there was a very small **Arctic tern** breeding colony near Everett (*BirdWeb*), which led to the occasional sighting of this species throughout the inland marine waters. Now this species is only known to occur pelagically off the Washington coast, and thus is even more unlikely to make an appearance near

San Juan Island. **Elegant terns** occasionally visit Washington, though usually on the outer coast. In July and August of 1992 there was an exceptionally large invasion to western Washington and elegant terns were seen in the San Juan Islands during this time (*WOS News* 21). The **pomarine and long-tailed jaeger** are regularly seen in the Strait of Juan de Fuca and very infrequently come further east towards the San Juan Islands. Both of these rare jaeger species were seen near Friday Harbor in October 2000 (*WOS News* 74), and on three separate prior occasions in the 1970s and 80s (Lewis and Sharpe 1987).

Alcids

Common murre
Uria aalge
Common
Year-round
Sites: South Beach, The Westside, Reuben Tarte County Park
Notes: There are no murre breeding colonies near San Juan Island, so this species is relatively uncommon in the spring and summer with only single birds being seen. Starting in late summer, pairs of fledged chicks and male parents begin to be seen, with more birds moving into the area during the fall from Washington and Oregon breeding colonies to feed on herring throughout the

Common murre

winter. Common murres are another local marine bird species that has declined dramatically in recent decades, with an estimated decrease of up to 90% since the 1970s. Large flocks can still be seen in the Strait of Juan de Fuca. Murres are one of the most likely seabirds to become entangled in functional or derelict fishing nets, and there are records of thousands of them dying in such a manner near San Juan Island in the 1990s.

Pigeon guillemot
Cepphus columba
Common
Year-round
Sites: Friday Harbor, Cattle Point, The Westside
Notes: Pigeon guillemots feed on bottom-dwelling creatures, and hence are usually found in relatively shallow waters. They look drastically different in the winter compared to their all-black breeding plumage, but they maintain their distinct white wing-patch year-round. There has been a small breeding colony in the cove to the north of Lime Kiln Lighthouse for many years, which makes this one of the most reliable places to see pigeon guillemots on San Juan Island.

Marbled murrelet
Brachyramphus marmoratus
Uncommon
Year-round
Sites: American Camp, The Westside, Reuben Tarte County Park
Notes: Only about 5% of the marbled murrelet population lives south of British Columbia. The roughly 20,000 birds found in the Pacific Northwest are considered a distinct population segment and have been listed as threatened in Washington since 1992. The biggest threat to this population of murrelets, which is still experiencing a downward trend in population size, is the logging of the old growth forest habitat that they require to breed. Locally, the marbled murrelets that live in the inland waters of Washington nest in the forests of Olympic National Park on the Olympic Peninsula.

While some murrelets are here year-round, peak sightings around the San Juan Islands occur in July and August when non-breeding birds from other regions come here to feed. They are usually seen in pairs.

Ancient murrelet
Synthliboramphus antiquus
Rare
Winter
Sites: Cattle Point, South Beach
Notes: The ancient murrelet tends to be more pelagic than most of our other alcids, though it becomes more coastal and can head into inland waters to feed during the winter months. Being on a boat increases the odds of finding this species; the only place they are irregularly seen from shore is Cattle Point. They can be seen in scattered flocks from October into February. The San Juan Islands are located right at the southernmost end of the historic breeding range for ancient murrelets, and while a Washington nest site hasn't been documented since the 1920s they may still breed in the region in very small numbers. Indeed, in June 2005 an adult bird was seen with two juveniles in San Juan County (*WOS News* 102).

Cassin's auklet
Ptychoramphus aleuticus
Occasional
Summer
Sites: Cattle Point, South Beach, Reuben Tarte County Park
Notes: Cassin's auklets range along the entire west coast of North America, and while they used to be considered one of the most abundant breeding sea birds in Washington, the largest portion of the population is now found in British Columbia. Despite the close proximity of the San Juan Islands to BC, the species prefers more pelagic habitats and is more often encountered along the outer coast. They are most likely to be seen in inland waters during mid to late summer. Often only a single bird is seen, but

during exceptional invasion years, as in 2009, they occur in greater numbers.

Rhinoceros auklet
Cerorhinca monocerata
Common
Year-round
Sites: Cattle Point, The Westside, Reuben Tarte County Park
Notes: Rhinoceros auklets can be seen in the San Juan Islands at any time of year, but are far more abundant during the breeding season. On summer evenings just before dusk birds can be seen with multiple bait fish hanging out of their mouths as they collect food to bring back to their chicks. Adult auklets only return to their nesting burrows on nearby offshore islands under the cover of darkness to avoid attracting predators. From October-February most birds disperse to feed off the Pacific Coast, though a few remain in inland waters. More closely related to puffins than auklets, some think this species should be renamed the rhinoceros puffin. The rhinoceros auklet is one of the most abundant breeding sea birds in Washington. The estimated 60,000 birds found in the state represent more than 90% of the US population of rhinoceros auklets south of Alaska.

Rhinoceros auklet

Tufted puffin
Fratercula cirrhata
Rare
Summer
Sites: Cattle Point, South Beach
Notes: While never as common here as in the prime part of their range in Alaska, there used to be more than a dozen puffin colonies in inland Washington waters that hosted several hundred breeding birds. The population was relatively stable through the 1980s, but has declined sharply since then, with about 50% of historic breeding colonies throughout the state no longer active. Near the San Juans, only Protection and Smith Islands in the Strait of Juan de Fuca still host breeding birds. The main issues affecting the tufted puffin population at large are prey availability, rising ocean temperatures, and predator introduction to nesting islands.

Very rare alcids
Confirmed sightings of a **thick-billed murre** occurred in Haro Strait in December 1979 (Tweit and Paulson 1994) and October 2004 (Mlodinow and Aanerod 2008). In 1996 the **long-billed murrelet** was split from the marbled murrelet, and a published photograph of an August 1993 sighting near Lopez Island was the first state record for this species. (Mlodinow and Aanerod 2008). A **Kittlitz's murrelet** was seen near Friday Harbor in January 1974 (Tweit and Paulson 1994), and several possible sightings in San Juan County have occurred since then though none have been confirmed. A single record of a **horned puffin** occurred in July 1977 (Lewis and Sharpe 1987).

Pigeons and Doves

Rock pigeon
Columba livia
Common
Year-round
Sites: Friday Harbor, Roche Harbor

Notes: Ubiquitous in mainland cities, this introduced species has had a foothold in the San Juan Islands since the 1950s. They are primarily seen near the docks in Friday Harbor and Roche Harbor or in the nearby residential areas.

Band-tailed pigeon
Patagioenas fasciata
Uncommon
Summer
Sites: Mt. Finlayson, English Camp, Mt. Young and Mitchell Hill
Notes: While ample habitat exists for this species on the island, it is not regularly encountered. Formerly abundant, band-tailed pigeons declined dramatically in the early 20th century due to over-hunting. After receiving protection the population recovered, but band-tailed pigeons have been declining again in recent decades. It is unclear what is contributing to this decline; it may again be the result of hunting. In some areas along the Pacific coast band-tailed pigeons remain year-round (particularly in urban areas), but they are considered partial migrants and most regional birds head south to California in winter.

Eurasian collared-dove
Streptopelia decaocto
Common
Year-round
Sites: Friday Harbor, Cattle Point, Roadside birding
Notes: While the first county record for the species occurred in 2005, the Eurasian collared-dove didn't really start increasing in numbers on San Juan Island until 2010 when it established a permanent presence here. One of the most rapidly expanding bird species worldwide in the last 100 years, the Eurasian collared-dove gained a foothold in the United States after being introduced to the Bahamas and reaching Florida in 1974. Since then it has spread west and north across the continent, increasing dramatically in the state of Washington since 2005. While the impact of this species on native birds is not yet known, some suggest it is filling the niche

left vacant by the extinction of the passenger pigeon, and thus may do less harm to resident bird populations than other non-native species.

Mourning dove
Zenaida macroura
Rare
Year-round
Sites: Friday Harbor, Cattle Point, Roadside birding
Notes: This species, like most of the other doves and pigeons, is for some reason far more common on the mainland than here in the islands. Mourning doves used to be considered common on San Juan Island through at least the 1950s, but numbers have decreased to the point where the species isn't even reported on an annual basis. The on-island population seems to vary quite a bit from year to year.

Owls

Barn owl
Tyto alba
Uncommon
Year-round
Sites: Roadside birding
Notes: Barn owls are present in small numbers year-round. Suitable habitat for them, including barns to roost and nest in and fields to find rodent prey, is limited on San Juan Island.

Western screech-owl
Megascops kennicottii
Uncommon
Year-round
Sites: Friday Harbor, Mt. Finlayson, Roadside birding
Notes: Pairs of western screech-owls are resident on their territories year-round, but can be very secretive and hard to detect. Slight declines throughout their range may be caused by predation by the

newly arrived barred owl. Their call, a series of short whistles that increase in rapidity, is diagnostic.

Great horned owl
Bubo virginianus
Uncommon
Year-round
Sites: Mt. Finlayson, Limekiln Preserve, Mt. Young and Mitchell Hill
Notes: This highly adaptable owl has increased in numbers throughout Washington State and may out-compete other owl species, though it seems to have declined in abundance on San Juan Island over recent years. One theory is that with expanded development on the island, great horned owls aren't able to find large enough territories here. They have likely also suffered from the decline of one of their main prey items on the island: rabbits.

Snowy owl
Bubo scandiacus
Occasional
Winter
Sites: South Beach, American Camp
Notes: During irruption years, a lack of voles and lemmings on its more northern haunts causes the snowy owl to expand its winter range south into the northwestern United States. They sometimes visit San Juan Island during these invasion seasons, which generally occur every 5-7 years. The most recent sighting on record is in December 2006 at American Camp (*WOS News* 111).

Barred owl
Strix varia
Uncommon
Year-round
Sites: Mt. Finlayson, Limekiln Preserve, Mt. Young and Mitchell Hill

Notes: This species used to be extremely rare in the San Juan Islands, but it has experienced a population expansion in the Pacific Northwest. The first Washington record occurred in 1965 and the first San Juan County record in 1981. The species started being regularly seen on San Juan Island during the 2000s and it is now a year-round breeding resident. Throughout much of its range the barred owl is starting to displace the spotted owl, perhaps in part because the former species is tolerant of second-growth forests while the latter prefers old-growth forests. With the San Juan Islands being almost entirely second-growth, it is no surprise that the spotted owl is not an expected species here. Listen for the distinct "who cooks for you?" call of the barred owl.

Short-eared owl
Asio flammeus
Uncommon
Winter
Sites: Cattle Point, South Beach, American Camp
Notes: Nomadic in the winter months, short-eared owls are most often seen on San Juan Island from January through April at dusk and dawn over the prairies at the south end of the island.

Northern saw-whet owl
Aegolius acadicus
Rare
Year-round
Sites: Mt. Finlayson, Limekiln Preserve, Mt. Young and Mitchell Hill
Notes: A resident of the north, with much of the population breeding in the boreal forests of Canada and Alaska or in the mountain ranges of the Lower 48, the northern saw-whet owl is in fact an infrequent nester on San Juan Island. While only a few birds may remain on the island during a given year, the species briefly becomes more common during migration.

Very rare owls

Northern pygmy-owls have been recorded at least three times in San Juan County: on Lopez Island in 2009 (Gayle Benton, pers. comm.), on Lopez Island in August 2001 (*WOS News* 79), and on Orcas Island in March 1983 (Lewis and Sharpe 1987). **Burrowing owls** have also been reported on a handful of occasions, most recently at American Camp in April 2004 (*WOS News* 101). The first San Juan County record of a **spotted owl** occurred in September 2007 on Sucia Island (Bartels County Firsts 2010). **Long-eared owls** are not expected to occur on San Juan Island, though twice (in 1987 and 2010, Lewis and Sharpe 1987 and Shona Aiken, pers. comm.) birds of this species have been found on the island and have had be taken to the Wolf Hollow Wildlife Rehabilitation Center.

Nighthawks and Swifts

Common nighthawk
Chordeiles minor
Uncommon
Summer
Sites: American Camp, Mt. Young and Mitchell Hill, Roadside Birding (Wold Road)
Notes: Any open habitat is a place to look for nighthawks, with birds foraging for flying insects at dusk and dawn and males giving impressive aerial flight displays during the breeding season. Nighthawks can be seen on San Juan Island from June through September. Several local birders report regularly seeing nighthawks during Island Stage Left's summer outdoor Shakespeare productions held on Wold Road.

Black swift
Cypseloides niger
Rare
Summer
Sites: Cattle Point, Roadside Birding

Notes: Very little is known about this high-flying species, with even its range yet to be firmly established. While it occurs regularly in the summer throughout southwestern British Columbia and northwest Washington, breeding locations within this region are for the most part unknown. It generally prefers higher elevations, but may head lower during periods of stormy weather. Its notched tail helps distinguish it from the Vaux's swift.

Vaux's swift
Chaetura vauxi
Uncommon
Summer
Sites: Cattle Point, Roadside birding
Notes: Look for the rapid flight of the Vaux's swift as it forages for insects from May through September, when breeding birds spread out to nest in forest habitat throughout Washington. Large groups of Vaux's swifts were reported over Friday Harbor in May 2011, leading to speculation that they may be beginning to roost here.

Hummingbirds

Anna's hummingbird
Calypte anna
Uncommon
Year-round
Sites: Friday Harbor, English Camp, Roche Harbor
Notes: Anna's hummingbirds first colonized the San Juan Islands in the 1980s during a period that saw this species experience a northward range expansion. By 2007, the Anna's hummingbird became an expected year-round resident. This hardy species survives Pacific Northwest winters by feeding on insects and sap in place of nectar and going into a state of torpor during cold nights. Ornamental flowers and feeders put out by humans help too. Sometimes this species will actually follow a red-breasted sapsucker intending to feed on the fruits of the woodpecker's labor. Any hummingbird seen in the fall or winter is undoubtedly an

Anna's, as our only other hummingbird species, the rufous, departs by the end of summer.

Rufous hummingbird
Selasphorus rufus
Common
Summer
Sites: Friday Harbor, English Camp, Roche Harbor
Notes: Rufous hummingbirds are most notable when they arrive in the spring, a time when males perform aerial flight displays for females and aggressively pursue any intruder into their breeding territory, including humans. Listen for their irritating, buzzing call. They tend to arrive as soon as flowers such as red-flowering currant and salmonberry are in bloom, generally early April, and they are one of the earliest departing migratory birds, leaving just after the breeding season ends in the height of summer. Numbers start to noticeably decline by August.

Rufous hummingbird

Kingfishers

Belted kingfisher
Ceryle alcyon
Common
Year-round
Sites: Jackson's Beach, Jakle's Lagoon, The Westside
Notes: Kingfishers are noisy residents of our coastlines and can often be detected by the chattering call they give in flight. During the breeding season look for pairs of kingfishers near their nesting sites: burrows into sandy cliff sides. In the winter, males and females separate and have their own territories, but remain in the region.

Belted kingfisher

Woodpeckers

Lewis' woodpecker
Melanerpes lewis
Occasional
Migration
Sites: American Camp, English Camp, Mt. Young and Mitchell Hill
Notes: Lewis' woodpeckers used to occur regularly in western Washington during summer months and were sometimes spotted on San Juan Island, but their numbers have declined with the arrival of the European starling (which out-compete them for

nesting cavities in trees) and the loss of their preferred habitat, which locally was Garry oak prairie. They are now considered very rare migrants in this part of the state, and hence are even more occasional on San Juan Island. One occurred near False Bay in May 2002 (Debby Clausen, pers. comm.). Another was seen at American Camp in August 1998 (*WOS News* 59).

Red-breasted sapsucker
Sphyrapicus ruber
Uncommon
Year-round
Sites: English Camp, Mt. Young and Mitchell Hill, Roche Harbor Highlands
Notes: The only sapsucker species seen on San Juan Island, the red-breasted sapsucker can be found year-round in coniferous forest habitats. They drill neat rows of holes into trees that act as wells that fill up with sap. The sap attracts insects, which they also feed on. Particularly in the winter they may be trailed by a resourceful Anna's hummingbird that will take advantage of the sap-filled holes these woodpeckers leave behind.

Downy woodpecker
Picoides pubescens
Common
Year-round
Sites: Friday Harbor, Cattle Point, English Camp
Notes: Usually seen in pairs throughout the year, these woodpeckers prefer to hang out in mixed forests and riparian habitats rather than dense forests. They can be easily confused with the similar but larger hairy woodpecker.

Hairy woodpecker
Picoides villosus
Common
Year-round
Sites: Friday Harbor, English Camp, Mt. Young and Mitchell Hill

Notes: Hairy woodpeckers, which tend to prefer coniferous woods as opposed to the mixed woodlands the downys inhabit, are probably outnumbered locally by their smaller cousins. On the island they overlap in habitat more than elsewhere.

Northern flicker
Colaptes auratus
Common
Year-round
Sites: Cattle Point, American Camp, English Camp
Notes: Northern flickers have a unique habit among woodpeckers in that they often sit on the ground to gather insects. Their call is striking, but somewhat softer than that of the pileated woodpecker. Virtually all of the flickers seen in the San Juan Islands are of the "red-shafted" race, distinct from the "yellow-shafted" race by having a gray face, brown crown, red mustache, and red wing

Northern flicker

linings. Intergrades between the two races may be seen in the fall and winter when more birds come here from elsewhere.

Pileated woodpecker
Dryocopus pileatus
Uncommon
Year-round
Sites: Mt. Finlayson, Limekiln Preserve, English Camp
Notes: The loud "wuk-wuk-wuk-wuk-wuk" call of the pileated woodpecker is one of the most extraordinary sounds that can be heard in local forests. This species seems slightly more common on the islands than on the mainland, though every encounter with this large, prehistoric-looking bird with its flaming red crest is a delight. Pairs defend large territories throughout the year, so seeing more than two birds at a time is rare unless the family has fledglings with them.

Very rare woodpeckers
Red-naped sapsuckers have been seen twice in the county: once on Orcas Island in April 2008 (*WOS News* 119) and once on San Juan Island in September 1985 (Lewis and Sharpe 1987). The only county record of a **white-headed woodpecker** was on Orcas Island in April 1995 (*WOS News* 39).

Flycatchers

Olive-sided flycatcher
Contopus cooperi
Common
Summer
Sites: American Camp, Limekiln Preserve, Mt. Young and Mitchell Hill
Notes: This bird is most easily located when giving its distinct "whip-three-beers" call from the very top of a coniferous tree. Currently listed as a species of concern by the US Fish and Wildlife Service and Audubon Washington, the species has experienced

declines in recent years for unknown reasons. Sightings in the islands are at their peak from late May through early August.

Western wood-pewee
Contopus sordidulus
Rare
Summer
Sites: American Camp, Limekiln Preserve, Roche Harbor Highlands
Notes: Despite the San Juan Islands being in the rain shadow of the Olympic Mountains and thus being having a more arid climate than many other parts of western Washington, the western wood-pewee tends to prefer even drier habitats than those found here. While more likely to be seen during migration, look for the occasional breeding pair from May through August.

Willow flycatcher
Empidonax trailli
Uncommon
Summer
Sites: American Camp, Limekiln Preserve, Mt. Young and Mitchell Hill
Notes: Aside from the Pacific-slope flycatcher, this is the most common of the other Empidonax flycatchers to be detected on San Juan Island. Noted for it's "fitz-bew" call, it is most often heard during the height of summer. It has a relatively late arrival for a breeding resident, not showing up until June.

Hammond's flycatcher
Empidonax hammondii
Rare
Summer
Sites: Limekiln Preserve, English Camp, Mt. Young and Mitchell Hill
Notes: Once common throughout western Washington, the Hammond's flycatcher prefers the old growth forest habitats that were mostly logged in the region during the first half of the 20th

century. As a result, the species is now more common further to the north where more old growth habitat remains intact, and they are relatively rare on San Juan Island and throughout this part of the state. Hammond's flycatchers also spend most of their time in the canopy of the forest, making them difficult to detect unless by call.

Pacific-slope flycatcher
Empidonax difficilis
Common
Summer
Sites: Limekiln Preserve, English Camp, Mt. Young and Mitchell Hill
Notes: Like other Empidonax flycatchers, the Pacific-slope flycatcher (known as the western flycatcher until the species split into the Pacific-slope and Cordilleran flycatchers in 1989) is most easily distinguished by call. In the spring and summer it can be heard giving it's high-pitched, two-note "su-weet" call throughout the island. They are usually found from the beginning of May through August.

Pacific-slope flycatcher

Western kingbird
Tyrannus verticalus
Occasional
Summer
Sites: Cattle Point, South Beach, American Camp
Notes: Western kingbirds, despite their name, are far more common in eastern Washington, but they do migrate in small numbers through the western part of the state. Additionally, with known breeding records in nearby Skagit County, it makes sense that this species occasionally visits the San Juan Islands, most recently in May 2011 when the author saw one at Cattle Point. A kingbird was also seen in 2010 (Kathleen Foley, pers. comm.) and two were seen at American Camp in August 1995 (*WOS News* 41).

Very rare flycatchers
The only county record for the **dusky flycatcher** was in Friday Harbor in April 2000 (*WOS News* 70). Lewis and Sharpe (1987) report three accounts of **Say's phoebes**; additionally, this species was seen at American camp in April 2008 (*WOS News* 119). An **ash-throated flycatcher** was seen on Lopez Island in July 2001 (*WOS News* 79). The only previous published county record for this species was on Orcas Island in September 1979 (Lewis and Sharpe 1987). There have been two unconfirmed sightings of **eastern kingbirds** in the county: one in July 2010 on San Juan Island (*eBird*) and one on Orcas Island in the summer of 1979 (Lewis and Sharpe 1987).

Shrikes

Northern shrike
Lanius excubitor
Uncommon
Winter
Sites: South Beach, American Camp, Roadside Birding
Notes: Abundance of this species varies from year to year; some seasons individuals stay further north, and others they roam

further south. The hooked bill of the shrike gives it away as a predator. Although smaller and lacking the talons of a raptor, shrikes feed on small birds, mice, and large insects. Look for them sitting on a prominent perch from mid-October through mid-April.

Vireos

Cassin's vireo
Vireo cassinii
Uncommon
Summer
Sites: American Camp, English Camp, Mt. Young and Mitchell Hill
Notes: The Cassin's vireo is one of three species that resulted from the splitting of the solitary vireo in 1997. Their susceptibility to brood parasitism from the brown-headed cowbird has kept them listed as a Species of Concern in Washington, though their numbers have increased in the last 20 years. The preference of this species for drier habitats makes San Juan Island an ideal place for it. The song of the Cassin's vireo is distinct: each separate note either inflects upward or downward, sounding like an endless series of questions and answers. They are most likely to be heard at the end of April and in early May.

Hutton's vireo
Vireo huttoni
Uncommon
Year-round
Sites: English Camp, Mt. Young and Mitchell Hill, Roche Harbor Trails
Notes: This species likely goes under-detected in part because of its elusive habits, but also because it looks similar to a ruby-crowned kinglet. It is the only vireo found on San Juan Island year-round, and is most easily detected in the winter among large mixed flocks of woodland passerines. During the spring and summer the song of the Hutton's vireo reveals its presence; listen for the repeated rising "zu-wee?"

Hutton's vireo

Warbling vireo
Vireo gilvus
Uncommon
Summer
Sites: American Camp, English Camp, Mt. Young and Mitchell Hill
Notes: The warbling vireo often forages for insects while hidden deep within the branches of deciduous trees and shrubs; learn their short, musical song and you are far more likely to detect them. This is the most commonly encountered vireo on the island in the spring. They arrive by the end of April.

Very rare vireos
Red-eyed vireos are usually found in eastern Washington, though they do breed in some western Washington river valleys including the nearby Skagit. With another small reported breeding population on Vancouver Island, it makes sense that bird would occasionally be seen in the San Juan Islands. There are three published reports of red-eyed vireos between 1984-1986, all documented in Lewis and Sharpe (1987).

Corvids

Northwestern crow
Corvus caurinus
Abundant
Year-round
Sites: Friday Harbor, False Bay and False Bay Drive, Roadside birding
Notes: While still officially listed as a separate species, many ornithologists believe that the northwestern crow is a sub-species of the American crow, Corvus brachyrhynchos. Both are found in western Washington and often associate together, and while the northwestern crow is supposedly smaller in size with a hoarser voice, they are generally considered indistinguishable in the field. Both types of crow overlap substantially in range, though consensus is that only northwestern crows inhabit San Juan Island.

The crows that gather in Friday Harbor can sometimes point a birder towards a more elusive species: they will call and dive-bomb a predator in flight or hidden in the trees. The target is often a raven, eagle, hawk, or owl. Watch out for the crafty crows at Lime Kiln Point State Park that use their cleverness to steal from picnickers. Not only will they readily swoop in to an untended feast while whale-watchers flock to the shoreline, but they have also learned how to open ziplock bags and even zippers on backpacks to get at food.

Common raven
Corvus corax
Common
Year-round
Sites: Mt. Finlayson, English Camp, Roche Harbor Trails
Notes: The raucous common raven seems particularly fond of the habitat in the northern part of the island, where their gurgling calls provide a constant sound track to any hike through the Roche Harbor trails. They remain year-round, but become noticeably more silent during the nesting season.

Very rare corvids

For those familiar with birding on the mainland in western Washington, it comes as a bit of a surprise to learn there are no jays on San Juan Island. **Steller's jays** are seen on Orcas Island but thus far have not colonized most of the other San Juans; one theory for this is because jays are poor flyers and don't like to cross open water. There have been occasional reports of single birds on San Juan Island, most recently in April 2006 (*WOS News* 107), but a population has yet to become established. There are two county records for **blue jays**, most recently in February 2004 on Orcas Island (*WOS News* 101). The other was in 1966 (Lewis and Sharpe 1987). There is one county sighting of a **gray jay** on San Juan Island in February 1975 (Lewis and Sharpe 1987). **Clark's nutcrackers** are periodically reported on Orcas Island, most recently in October 2008 (*WOS News* 123). **A black-billed magpie** was seen on San Juan Island by Thor Hanson in April 2011 (Barb Jensen, pers. comm.); the only other time this species was seen in San Juan County was in 1983 on Orcas Island (Lewis and Sharpe 1987).

Larks and Swallows

Horned lark
Eremophila alpestris
Occasional
Migration
Sites: Cattle Point, South Beach, American Camp
Notes: The horned lark used to breed on the prairies at the south end of the island but it has been locally extirpated due to factors such as increased predation from introduced species like the red fox and feral cats and degradation of the prairie habitat it relies on. With the current restoration efforts that are an ongoing project at American Camp, it's possible this species could return to the island in the future, but currently it may only be rarely seen during migration, particularly September. The horned lark is currently listed as Endangered in the state of Washington.

Purple martin
Progne subis
Rare
Summer
Sites: Cattle Point, English Camp, Roche Harbor
Notes: Purple martins have declined significantly over the last 60 years, due in part to being out-competed by the non-native European starling for nesting cavities. Martins now only breed in very localized areas, particularly in places starlings shun like over water and in specialized nest boxes. A few individuals breed on San Juan Island from time to time, most often in the nest boxes at the Roche Harbor marina. They may be encountered elsewhere on the island during migration. Another reliable place to see this species locally is at the summer breeding colony on the abandoned dock pilings in the cove next to the Anacortes ferry terminal.

Tree swallow
Tachycineta bicolor
Common
Summer
Sites: Sportsman's and Egg Lakes, Roadside Birding
Notes: Tree swallows are one of the earliest arriving summer migrants, in part because they don't travel as far south as other species and also because they will eat seeds and berries if there aren't enough insects yet to sustain them. They sometimes start showing up in late February, and increase in numbers by the end of March. They are also one of our earliest departing swallows, usually leaving the area by mid-August.

Violet-green swallow
Tachycineta thalassina
Abundant
Summer
Sites: Limekiln Preserve, Sportsman's and Egg Lakes, Roadside Birding

Tree swallow

Notes: Violet-green swallows have experienced population growth over recent decades, making them one of the most abundant swallow species on San Juan Island. They are expected to arrive by the end of March, and continue swooping over lakes, ponds, and other open areas for insects until early September.

Northern rough-winged swallow
Stelgidopteryx serripennis
Common
Summer
Sites: Fourth of July Beach, Jakle's and Third Lagoons, English Camp
Notes: Northern rough-winged swallows tend to arrive later and leave earlier than the other swallow species; they are most likely to be seen on San Juan Island from mid-April through the end of August. They rarely occur in large congregations as the other swallow species do, but can be seen mixed in with larger flocks of other swallows.

Cliff swallow
Petrochelidon pyrrhonota
Uncommon
Summer
Sites: American Camp, Sportsman's and Egg Lakes, Roadside birding
Notes: Cliff swallows, as their name suggests, originally built their mud nests only on the faces of cliffs. They have taken advantage of man-made structures, however, to expand their range, and will also build their nests on buildings and under bridges. On San Juan Island, they take advantage of the natural cliff faces on the west side of the island, though they're also seen with other swallow species over lakes and ponds. Look for them from April through August.

Barn swallow
Hirundo rustica
Abundant
Summer
Sites: Cattle Point, The Westside, Roadside birding
Notes: Barn swallows are the most widespread swallow species on San Juan Island, and along with the violet-green swallow are the most abundant. They arrive somewhat later than most other swallow species (generally in mid-April) and are the last ones to depart, remaining well into September. Every few years one or two are even reported over-wintering in San Juan County. Their deeply forked tails help differentiate them from other swallow species.

Very rare larks and swallows
From 1960-2000 American Camp on San Juan Island was known for its **Eurasian skylarks**, a species that established a small colony here after being introduced to Vancouver Island. The last breeding record was in 1999 and the last confirmed sighting in 2000 (*WOS News* 74), and the species is now considered extirpated. A **bank swallow** was reported at American Camp in July 1995 (*WOS News* 40), and other unconfirmed reports have occurred throughout the years.

Chickadees, Bushtits, Creepers, and Nuthatches

Chestnut-backed chickadee
Poecile rufescens
Abundant
Year-round
Sites: The Westside (Lime Kiln Point State Park), English Camp, Roche Harbor Trails
Notes: Outnumbered on the mainland by the black-capped chickadee, the chestnut-backed is the sole chickadee representative on San Juan Island. Because they have declined in the Seattle area, chestnut-backed chickadees are considered a species at risk in the state of Washington, but populations have increased or remained stable elsewhere in the state, and they flat-out thrive on San Juan Island.

Chestnut-backed chickadee

Bushtit
Psaltriparus minimus
Common
Year-round
Sites: Fourth of July Beach, Mt. Finlayson, English Camp
Notes: In the winter bushtits gather in flocks and can be seen vivaciously flying from one stand of scrub brush to the next. In the

spring they pair off and build hanging nests out of lichen and moss, and simultaneously become more difficult to detect throughout the rest of the breeding season. Bushtits didn't historically inhabit the San Juan Islands but first spread here during the 1930s, probably due to the increase in open and second growth forest habitat availability that coincided with major logging operations at the time. While they now inhabit most of western Washington, they are still absent from most of the Olympic Peninsula where the dense temperate rainforest remains intact.

Red-breasted nuthatch
Sitta canadensis
Common
Year-round
Sites: Mt. Finlayson, Limekiln Preserve, Roche Harbor Highlands
Notes: The nasal "yang, yang, yang" call of the red-breasted nuthatch can be heard on nearly every excursion into coniferous forest habitat. During the winter they join forces with flocks of chickadees and other woodland passerines, always a delightful "pocket" of species for a birder to happen upon. While they are common here throughout the year, in the winter additional birds from Alaska, Canada, and the regional mountain ranges join the local population.

Brown creeper
Certhia americana
Common
Year-round
Sites: Limekiln Preserve, English Camp, Roche Harbor Highlands
Notes: While large winter congregations of winter passerines are predominantly made up of chickadees and kinglets, close examination can usually yield one or two creepers near the outskirts of the flock. These birds, well-camouflaged against the tree bark, work their way up a tree, then fly down to the bottom of the next tree.

Very rare chickadees
Black-capped chickadees don't like to fly over water more than
0.75 miles wide, which has kept them from colonizing the San Juan
Islands or Vancouver Island (*WOS News* 18). Sporadic reports of
individual birds continue to occur in San Juan County every few
years, but apparently not in great enough numbers for this species
to become established on the islands. Many birders erroneously
assume the chickadees they see here are black-cappeds, which
makes it difficult to confirm many of the reported sightings.

Red-breasted nuthatch

Wrens and Dippers

Bewick's wren
Thryomanes bewickii
Uncommon
Year-round
Sites: Friday Harbor, American Camp, English Camp
Notes: While this species is declining in the eastern part of its
range, it is thriving along the west coast, including in western
Washington. They are often seen in pairs throughout the year.

House wren
Troglodytes aedon
Common
Summer
Sites: Limekiln Preserve, English Camp, Mt. Young and Mitchell Hill
Notes: The slightly drier habitat found on San Juan Island as a result of being in the rain shadow of the Olympic Mountains results in the island being an attractive site for house wrens. They are more common here than elsewhere in western Washington, and generally arrive at the end of April or in early May. Numbers start to dwindle by the end of August.

Pacific wren
Troglodytes pacificus
Common
Year-round
Sites: Mt. Finlayson, Limekiln Preserve, Mt. Young and Mitchell Hill
Notes: In 2010 the winter wren was split into three different species: the Pacific wren in western North America, the winter wren in eastern North America, and the Eurasian wren in the Old World. Locally, Pacific wrens are most abundant in the winter when birds that breed in the nearby mountain ranges head to lower elevations. Some birds do remain here to breed, and have been known to take advantage of nest boxes.

Marsh wren
Cistothorus palustris
Common
Year-round
Sites: Sportsman's and Egg Lakes, Roadside birding
Notes: Despite a relative lack of the extensive cattail marsh habitat preferred by this species, it occurs in most roadside marshlands on San Juan Island. The staccato call may give away its presence at any time of year, though it sings almost constantly in the spring when

it is most easily detected. In the winter, some birds may roam away from the flooded marshes to damp fields with dense grass.

Very rare wrens and dippers
Primarily a species that occurs east of the Cascades, the **rock wren** sporadically migrates through western Washington and was historically noted as a breeder in the San Juan Islands. While more likely to occur in more appropriate habitat on Orcas Island in places like Mt. Constitution, the rock wren used to be noted with regularity near Mt. Dallas on San Juan Island. In May 2011 Matt Bartels spotted one at South Beach (*Tweeters* e-mail report) The **American dipper** is occasionally reported on Orcas Island along some of the lakes and streams (Gayle Benton, pers. comm.).

Kinglets

Golden-crowned kinglet
Regulus satrapa
Common
Winter
Sites: Mt. Finlayson, The Westside (Lime Kiln Point State Park), Roche Harbor Highlands
Notes: The golden-crowned kinglet is far more abundant during the winter when seen in large mixed flocks with other small woodland birds. The high-pitched call of this restless bird will often alert a birder that a flock of kinglets is there, but getting one to sit still enough for a good look through binoculars is another task entirely. Many birds head north to breed, and those few that remain become secretive.

Ruby-crowned kinglet
Regulus calendula
Uncommon
Winter
Sites: Mt. Finlayson, English Camp, Roche Harbor Highlands

Notes: Ruby-crowned kinglets are easily confused with the similar Hutton's vireo. In addition to other field marks like a thinner beak and black behind the wing bars, look for the constant twitching of the tail and wing flicks associated with the more petite kinglet. During especially cold winters these birds may migrate further south and be less abundant. Look for them in mixed species flocks during winter. In the summer they head to Alaska, British Columbia, or higher altitudes to breed. Occasionally small numbers breed locally.

Thrushes and Thrashers

Western bluebird
Sialia mexicana
Uncommon
Year-round
Sites: American Camp, Roadside birding
Notes: Formerly common on San Juan Island, this species went locally extinct in the 1960s with the expansion of the European starling, with which it competes for nesting sites, and the decline of the Garry oak habitat it depends on. A reintroduction project started in 2006 has successfully brought this species back as a breeder on the island. Birds are spread out into breeding pairs during the summer, but gather into larger flocks in the fall and small numbers sometimes spend the entire winter here. The best places to look for them are on the rural roads through San Juan Valley including Douglas and Bailer Hill Roads and Valley Farms Road. They are also reported at American Camp and near San Juan Vineyards on Roche Harbor Road.

Mountain bluebird
Sialia currucoides
Uncommon
Migration
Sites: Mt. Finlayson, South Beach

Notes: This species is more commonly found east of the Cascades, but a few birds migrate west of the Cascades and sometimes single birds or small flocks stop over on San Juan Island on their way through to their high elevation nesting sites as far north as Alaska. Sightings are most likely to occur in March through May or August into November.

Townsend's solitaire
Myadestes townsendi
Migration
Winter
Sites: Mt. Finlayson, The Westside (Lime Kiln Point State Park), Mt. Young and Mitchell Hill
Notes: Generally preferring higher altitude habitats, the Townsend's solitaire is most likely observed during migration: March-April and August-September. They sometimes over-winter here as well, with one being detected during the Christmas Bird Count every few years. Look for them either along stretches of forested shoreline, or in some of the island's higher elevation areas such as the woods on Mt. Young and Mitchell Hill.

Swainson's thrush
Catharus ustulatus
Common
Summer
Sites: American Camp, Mt. Young and Mitchell Hill, Sportsman's and Egg Lakes
Notes: The melodious ascending song of the Swainson's thrush is one of the true harbingers of summer on San Juan Island. In the fall, these birds literally depart overnight, as migration occurs under the cover of darkness. Look for the western russet-backed sub-species on San Juan Island, though in reality this species may never be seen, only heard.

Hermit thrush
Catharus guttatus
Uncommon
Winter
Sites: English Camp, Mt. Young and Mitchell Hill, Roche Harbor Trails
Notes: These altitudinal migrants breed in the Cascade and Olympic Mountain ranges and winter in the lowlands including on San Juan Island.

American robin
Turdus migratorius
Abundant
Year-round
Sites: Cattle Point, American Camp, English Camp
Notes: While the species is present at any time of year, the American robin is actually a migratory species, so we see different individuals here in the summer than in the winter. The different populations of robins are poorly understood, but they are always abundant on the island.

Varied thrush
Ixoreus naevius
Common
Winter
Sites: Limekiln Preserve, English Camp, Roche Harbor Highlands
Notes: Varied thrushes are most abundant in the winter when birds from nearby mountain ranges descend to sea level for the duration of the colder weather. Some birds stay and breed on the island, but fewer than in years past due to more fragmented forest habitat. Listen for their distinct call, a loud monotone whistle.

Very rare thrashers
In June 1995 a **brown thrasher** was seen at American Camp, the only county record for this species (Aanerud and Mattocks 1997).

Starlings

European starling
Sturnus vulgaris
Abundant
Year-round
Sites: Cattle Point, American Camp, Roadside birding
Notes: After being introduced into New York City's Central Park in 1890, the European starling reached western Washington by 1950 and became abundant by the 1970s. While their population has remained relatively constant since then, they are considered an invasive species since they out-compete many native cavity-nesting species for breeding sites. They gather in large flocks during the winter. These mimics replicate the vocalizations of a wide range of local species, sounding like everything from a red-winged blackbird to a red-tailed hawk to a killdeer. Be wary of identifying birds by call when starlings are nearby.

Pipits and Accentors

American pipit
Anthus rubescens
Uncommon
Migration
Sites: South Beach, False Bay and False Bay Drive, Roadside birding
Notes: Heavily streaked and almost resembling sparrows except for their thin bills, American pipits can easily go unnoticed in the grassy habitat they prefer. Becoming familiar with their vocalizations can help to locate them. Look for loose flocks of this species in open areas during April and May in the spring and September through November in the fall. One popular place to look for pipits is near the parking area at South Beach, though they can pop up in unexpected places as well like near the airport in Friday Harbor.

Very rare pipits

A **Siberian accentor** was reported on Orcas Island in January 1991 (Mlodinow and Aanerod 2008). In September 1979, a **red-throated pipit** spent three days with a migrating flock of American pipits (Tweit and Paulson 1994). This was the first Washington record of this species.

Cedar waxwing

Waxwings

Cedar waxwing
Bombycilla cedrorum
Uncommon
Year-round
Sites: Friday Harbor, Cattle Point, English Camp
Notes: Winter range for the cedar waxwing is unpredictable, as they will remain resident or migrate depending on food availability. They are expected every year until at least September. While they will fly-catch insects and eat vegetation, berries are a favorite food item and any bush or tree with ripe fruit, such as juniper or madrone, could host a whole flock of waxwings.

Very rare waxwings

There is a single published record of a **Bohemian waxwing** in with a flock of cedar waxwings on Orcas Island in June 1983 (Lewis and Sharpe 1987). It is more typical for these boreal waxwings to venture into Washington in winter when northern breeders head south, but there has also been documented breeding in the North Cascades in nearby Whatcom County, so it's possible for this species to visit again at any time of year.

Longspurs and Buntings

Lapland longspur
Calcarius lapponicus
Occasional
Migration
Sites: Cattle Point, South Beach, American Camp
Notes: Since the 1970s, reports of this species have declined in western Washington. Like other species such as the horned lark, the Lapland longspur has suffered the consequences of the degradation of the prairie habitat that they rely on. While occasional visits still occur, most often at the south end of the island, it's not unusual for years to go by between sightings.

Snow bunting
Plectrophenax nivalis
Occasional
Winter
Sites: Cattle Point, South Beach, American Camp
Notes: Like the Lapland longspur, the snow bunting no longer visits the western part of Washington state as regularly as it did before the 1970s. Sporadic reports will still occur, but they are more often seen in eastern Washington during the winter.

Warblers

Orange-crowned warbler
Oreothylpus celata
Common
Summer
Sites: American Camp, The Westside, English Camp
Notes: The most common warbler on San Juan Island and one of the first to arrive in the spring, the drab orange-crowned warbler is probably most distinguishable by its relative lack of field marks. Olive-green overall with no wing-bars or eye ring and an orange crown that mostly remains hidden, orange-crowned warblers may seem to be a difficult bird to identify but they are actually distinct in their lack of markings. Regularly heard singing by early April, their staccato trill is similar to the song of the dark-eyed junco and the chipping sparrow, both of which are also found in the same habitats, so be careful when identifying this bird by ear alone.

MacGillivray's warbler
Geothlypis tolmiei
Occasional
Migration
Sites: Mt. Finlayson, American Camp, Limekiln Preserve
Notes: Far less common than it used to be, possibly due to brood parasitism by brown-headed cowbirds, the MacGillivray's warbler is no longer a confirmed nester on San Juan Island. They are most likely to be encountered during late April and May or in August and early September when they are migrating. The song of the MacGillivray's is a rolling series of five or six quick syllables that descends over the last two notes.

Common yellowthroat

Geothlypis trichas

Common

Summer

Sites: False Bay Drive (Panorama Marsh), Sportsman's and Egg Lakes, Roadside birding

Notes: Listen for the distinct "witchity-witchity-witch" song of the common yellowthroat at roadside wetlands from April through September. They are particularly fond of cattail marshes. Like the yellow warbler, yellowthroats have lived alongside cowbirds long enough to adapt mechanisms to avoid their brood parasitism.

Yellow warbler

Setophaga petechia

Uncommon

Summer

Sites: American Camp, English Camp, Sportsman's and Egg Lakes

Notes: The "sweet sweet sweet, I'm so sweet" song of the yellow warbler helps identify it when it remains secluded among the leaves and branches in its mixed woods habitat. Yellow warblers, having lived alongside brown-headed cowbirds in their native range, have developed a defense against their brood parasitism. When a cowbird lays eggs in a yellow warbler nest, they build another nest over the cowbird eggs. This has kept them from being as impacted by cowbirds as other similar species in the Pacific Northwest. They have typically arrived on the island by the beginning of May.

Yellow-rumped warbler

Setophaga coronata

Common

Summer

Sites: American Camp, Limekiln Preserve (Westside Lake), Sportsman's and Egg Lakes

Notes: In 1973 the myrtle and Audubon's warblers were lumped into a single species, the yellow-rumped warbler, based on evidence of hybridization. More recent genetic research indicates that the

Yellow-rumped warbler (Audubon's)

two different morphs of this species may in fact be reproductively isolated, but in 2011 the American Ornithological Union voted to keep them a single species rather than re-splitting them. The myrtle sub-species over-winters in Washington but breeds further to the north. Though they do visit the Islands in varying numbers in the winter months, they are most often encountered during migration as one of the earliest spring and latest fall migrants. Unlike the myrtle sub-species, the Audubon's sub-species departs northern Washington for the winter and returns to the region to breed in the early spring, and their song is one of the first indicators to birders that summer is just around the corner. The Audubon's morph remains common on San Juan Island throughout the summer. During migratory periods, mixed flocks of the two sub-species are seen, but in general winter birds will be the myrtle sub-species and summer birds will be Audubon's. Peak numbers of both species are generally reported in April and May, with another peak in September during the fall migration.

Black-throated gray warbler
Setophaga nigrescens
Uncommon
Summer
Sites: Limekiln Preserve, English Camp, Mt. Young and Mitchell Hill
Notes: Black-throated gray warblers have likely increased on San Juan Island, taking advantage of the mixed second growth woods that replaced the former old growth forest. The song is a buzzy "weezy-weezy-weezy-weezy-weezy-weez-eet", but those birding by ear should be aware that black-throated grays can sound a lot like Townsend's warblers. Normally these two species occupy different habitats, with the black-throated gray preferring more deciduous habitats and the Townsend's residing in coniferous woods, but their ranges overlap on the island. Black-throated gray warblers arrive in the San Juan Islands in mid-April and depart in September.

Townsend's warbler
Setophaga townsendi
Uncommon
Year-round
Sites: Limekiln Preserve, English Camp, Mt. Young and Mitchell Hill
Notes: Townsend's warblers are generally found at higher altitudes or in more coniferous habitats, but they are regular visitors in the mixed forests on the island. The warblers that breed here depart to Central America in the winter and are replaced by birds that migrate shorter distances to over-winter here from British Columbia. The song of the Townsend's is a series of about seven quick "zee" notes followed by a higher pitched "doo-dee-dee". While distinct, sometimes the song sounds similar to that of a black-throated gray warbler, with which it overlaps in habitat on the island.

Wilson's warbler
Cardellina pusilla
Uncommon
Summer
Sites: American Camp, Westside Lake, Sportsman's and Egg Lakes
Notes: Wilson's warblers are one of the most common warblers in western Washington, though a comparative lack of their preferred wet deciduous habitat on San Juan Island makes them uncommon here. They tend to be found in the scrub brush near ponds and lakes and one of the most accessible places to see them is near Westside Lake. They sound like a slowed down version of an orange-crowned warbler, with each note in the trill more distinct. Wilson's warblers are one of our latest arriving warblers, generally not showing up until May.

Wilson's warbler

Very rare warblers
Other warblers that occur irregularly in the county are (with most recent published sighting in parentheses, with source): **Tennessee warbler** (San Juan Island in September 1982, Tweit and Paulson 1994), **Nashville warbler** (Orcas Island 1986, Lewis and Sharpe 1987), **hermit warbler** (Lopez Island 2008, Gayle Benton pers. comm.), **palm warbler** (Cattle Point in November 2000, *WOS News*

74), **black-and-white warbler** (Orcas Island in May 1963, Lewis and Sharpe 1987), and **ovenbird** (Friday Harbor June 1983, Tweit and Skriletz 1996). Most of these warblers are most likely to be encountered during migration, except for the palm warbler, which occur in small numbers along the west coast in fall and winter.

Sparrows

Spotted towhee
Pipilo maculatus
Common
Year-round
Sites: Mt. Finlayson, English Camp, Roche Harbor Highlands
Notes: Often lurking in the middle of dense scrub brush, towhees can be located aurally by either their scratching through the organic detritus on the ground or by their vocalizations. They're questioning "Queee?" call is heard year-round, and their song is a distinct "Drink-your-tea-a-a-a". Formerly known as the rufous-sided towhee, a species split occurred in 1995 separating this species from the similar eastern towhee.

Spotted towhee

Chipping sparrow
Spizella passerina
Uncommon
Summer
Sites: Limekiln Preserve, English Camp, Mt. Young and Mitchell Hill
Notes: The chipping sparrow prefers the somewhat drier habitat that exists on San Juan Island, though it has experienced declines here and elsewhere in the state. It is currently considered a Washington Species At Risk. Main threats include loss of habitat and brown-headed cowbird parasitism, as well as competition with house sparrows (the latter threat may become less of a factor as house sparrows decline). Their song sounds similar to that of the dark-eyed junco and orange-crowned warbler.

Vesper sparrow
Pooecetes gramineus
Rare
Summer
Sites: South Beach, American Camp, Roadside birding
Notes: This species isn't nearly as common on San Juan Island as it was several decades ago; it is now listed as a Species of Concern in Washington. The affinis subspecies found west of the Cascades has been affected by the loss and degradation of the prairie habitat where it breeds. Another cause of their decline is the presence of feral cats, which easily prey upon this ground-nesting species. This is a known problem in their prime habitat areas on the island such as American Camp.

Savannah sparrow
Passerculus sandwichensis
Abundant
Summer
Sites: South Beach, American Camp, False Bay and False Bay Drive
Notes: The buzzing song of the savannah sparrow is one of the most common sounds heard in the grasslands at the south end of San

Juan Island, as well as throughout many of the agricultural areas in the interior of the island.

Fox sparrow
Passerella iliaca
Uncommon
Winter
Sites: Fourth of July Beach, Jakle's Lagoon, Roche Harbor Highlands
Notes: This highly variable species is made up of many races. The most common race observed on San Juan Island is the dark sooty fox sparrow, Passerella iliaca fuliginosa. This race may look far different from other red or gray races that birders from elsewhere are familiar with.

Song sparrow
Melospiza melodia
Common
Year-round
Sites: Fourth of July Beach, Mt. Finlayson, English Camp
Notes: This most abundant sparrow on the island can easily be seen in a wide variety of habitats throughout the year. Though their vocalizations are highly variable, listen for the two to four pure whistling notes that begin every song.

Song sparrow

Lincoln's sparrow
Melospiza lincolnii
Uncommon
Migration
Sites: Cattle Point, South Beach, American Camp
Notes: One of the rarer sparrows on San Juan Island, Lincoln's are most likely to be seen during migration (April-May and September-October), though a single individual may sometimes over-winter. Look for these secretive birds mixed in with other flocks of sparrows.

White-throated sparrow
Zonotrichia albicollis
Occasional
Winter
Sites: Friday Harbor, South Beach
Notes: Look for these rare winter visitors amid other flocks of sparrows, particularly white-crowned and golden-crowned sparrows. They may turn up at bird feeders from time to time.

White-crowned sparrow
Zonotrichia leucophrys
Abundant
Summer
Sites: Cattle Point, South Beach, The Westside
Notes: Biologists have extensively studied white-crowned sparrows in the Salish Sea region for their geographically-variable song dialects. The birds on San Juan Island sing a distinct "Oh me, pretty, pretty me" that can be heard throughout the summer. Occasionally seen in the winter as well, most birds head towards the outer coast and are replaced by their cousin golden-crowned sparrows. The birds that are seen here in the winter, generally in small numbers, have migrated from the north.

White-crowned sparrow

Golden-crowned sparrow
Zonotrichia atricapilla
Abundant
Winter
Sites: Fourth of July Beach, The Westside, Roadside birding
Notes: Our most common winter sparrow, golden-crowneds have increased in numbers throughout the last few decades. The large flocks we see on San Juan Island usually include a mixture of immatures and adults in winter plumage, and they can usually be found in any blackberry thicket. Before they depart in spring, they may start singing their mournful "Oh, dear, me" song that is more typically heard on their breeding grounds.

Dark-eyed junco
Junco hyemalis
Abundant
Year-round
Sites: The Westside (Lime Kiln Point State Park), English Camp, Roche Harbor Trails
Notes: In 1973, the various races of junco were combined into a single species, the dark-eyed junco. The Oregon race is the predominant

Dark-eyed junco

variety seen on San Juan Island, though the occasional slate-colored bird may also be seen. Note that the song of the dark-eyed junco is very similar to that of the chipping sparrow and orange-crowned warbler, and that on the island all three species can occur in the same habitat.

Very rare sparrows
An **American tree sparrow** was seen on Lopez Island in November 2007 (*WOS News* 116), the first time the species had been reported in the county since a 1955 Christmas Bird Count (Lewis and Sharpe 1987). **Lark sparrows** were seen twice on San Juan Island in 1983 and 1984 (Lewis and Sharpe 1987). The following sparrow species have been reported in San Juan County on a single occasion: a **clay-colored sparrow** was reported in June 2003 on Sucia Island (*WOS News* 90), and a single **black-throated sparrow** was on Henry Island in May 1987 (*WOS News* 47).

Tanagers and Grosbeaks

Western tanager
Piranga ludoviciana
Uncommon
Summer
Sites: English Camp, Mt. Young and Mitchell Hill, Sportsman's and Egg Lakes
Notes: Look for these bright-colored forest birds from May into early September. They are usually in pairs.

Black-headed grosbeak
Pheucticus melanocephalus
Uncommon
Summer
Sites: American Camp, Limekiln Preserve, English Camp
Notes: Our only regularly encountered grosbeak, the general consensus among local birders is that the black-headed grosbeak is increasing on the island and is now breeding here in greater numbers than in years past. They often remain hidden within trees, and their song sounds similar to that of the American robin, so it can be easy to miss this expected species. Black-headed grosbeaks are most closely related to sparrows, while the other grosbeaks sometimes seen on San Juan Island (the evening and the pine) are actually more closely related to finches, hence they are listed in different places in field guides and on bird lists.

Lazuli bunting
Passerina amoena
Occasional
Summer
Sites: Friday Harbor, American Camp, English Camp
Notes: Although primarily a species that occurs in eastern Washington, there are a few population segments of the Lazuli bunting west of the Cascades, including the nearby Skagit River Valley on the mainland. There are at least five records of this

species in San Juan County since 2000, all of them in either May or June (*eBird*, *WOS News* 72, 76, pers. comms.).

Very rare grosbeaks, and buntings
The first and only county record for a **rose-breasted grosbeak** was in September 1994 on Shaw Island (Aanerud and Mattocks 2000). **Indigo buntings** have been reported twice: in July 1984 (Tweit and Skriletz 1996) and May 1992 (Tweit and Paulson 1994), both on San Juan Island.

Blackbirds and Orioles

Red-winged blackbird
Agelaius phoeniceus
Common
Year-round
Sites: Cattle Point, Sportsman's and Egg Lakes, Roadside birding
Notes: Red-winged blackbirds will nest in even the smallest wetland habitat, so in addition to some of the Island's larger lakes look for them at any roadside pond or marsh. In the winter, large flocks congregate and often move away from the water into farmlands or the grasslands at the south end of the island.

Red-winged blackbird

Western meadowlark
Sturnella neglecta
Uncommon
Winter
Notes: A resident breeder until at least 1960, the western meadowlark is now a winter visitor only. The species has declined somewhat throughout western Washington due to the loss of the prairie habitat it depends upon.

Brewer's blackbird
Euphagus cyanocephalus
Common
Year-round
Sites: Cattle Point, Roadside birding
Notes: Brewer's blackbirds occur in smaller numbers than European starlings or red-winged blackbirds, though they are also here year-round. A regular place to see them is along Bailer Hill Road.

Brown-headed cowbird
Molothrus ater
Abundant
Summer
Sites: Cattle Point, American Camp, Roadside birding
Notes: The range of brown-headed cowbird, formerly a grassland species, has expanded to include much of the continent due to deforestation and other land clearing. Brown-headed cowbirds first colonized the San Juan Islands in the 1950s and it's no coincidence that many other local bird species started to decline shortly thereafter. Cowbirds lay their eggs in nests of as many as 200 other species, leaving their chicks to unsuspecting host birds of other species. Not only do the foster parents have to feed the cowbird chick, but the chick also ousts the native offspring. Particularly susceptible to cowbird brood parasitism are species like warblers, bluebirds, and sparrows. Peak cowbird numbers occur on San Juan Island from May through mid-August, though rarely one or two birds can be found in with other blackbird flocks during the winter.

Very rare blackbirds
A **bobolink** was seen in the county in July 1991 (Bartels County Firsts 2010). The **yellow-headed blackbird** is very occasionally seen on San Juan Island during the summer; there was one reported in May 2009 (Blake Hough, pers. comm.) and another in April 2006 (*WOS News* 107). **Bullock's orioles** have increased in western Washington in recent years and are considered fairly common around Puget Sound for a brief period during the summer. They have been infrequently reported in the San Juan Islands during this time, with the most recent sighting occurring in May 2006 on Orcas Island (*eBird*).

Finches

Purple finch
Carpodacus purpureus
Uncommon
Year-round
Sites: Fourth of July Beach, Cattle Point, American Camp
Notes: Purple finches have declined after the introduction of the non-native house sparrow and the expansion of the house finch, and their numbers fluctuate from year to year based on the availability of their preferred food: conifer seeds.

House finch
Carpodacus mexicanus
Common
Year-round
Sites: Friday Harbor, Cattle Point, American Camp
Notes: Native to the southwestern United States, the house finch didn't naturally expand its range to western Washington until the 1950s. This finch species thrives in human-altered habitats and is now our most abundant finch on San Juan Island.

Red crossbill
Loxia curvirostra
Uncommon
Year-round
Sites: Mt. Finlayson, Limekiln Preserve, Mt. Young and Mitchell Hill
Notes: A highly nomadic species, the red crossbill can be a difficult bird to pin down at any one location. There is ample habitat for them throughout San Juan Island, however, and despite their irruptive habits they are fairly regular here. While there may be unpredictable periods of several months when they are absent, they are expected and indeed will breed at any time of year. Becoming familiar with their "kip-kip-kip-kip" vocalizations will help you locate a flock foraging in the forest or flying overhead. There are many different types of crossbills that are best distinguished by vocalization; the predominant type of San Juan Island is Type 4 (*WOS News* 27), which prefers to feed on Douglas fir seeds.

Pine siskin
Spinus pinus
Uncommon
Year-round
Sites: Friday Harbor, Mt. Finlayson, Cattle Point
Notes: Pine siskins are a highly irruptive species and may occur in large flocks one year only to be nearly absent the next. Like crossbills and purple finches, they are dependent on coniferous cone crops.

American goldfinch
Carduelis tristis
Abundant
Summer
Sites: Friday Harbor, South Beach, American Camp
Notes: Another species that has thrived alongside the presence of humans, goldfinches have increased in western Washington as mixed forests have replaced old-growth coniferous forests. Their

favorite food is thistle seeds, so in addition to visiting bird feeders it's no surprise that they are common in the prairies at the south end of the island where thistles grow in abundance. The American goldfinch is the state bird of Washington.

American goldfinch

Evening grosbeak
Coccothraustes vespertinus
Rare
Year-round
Sites: Friday Harbor
Notes: Evening grosbeaks are another species susceptible to irruptions, hence their occurrence on the island is unpredictable. They wander widely, particularly in winter, and may be relatively common in Washington some years and entirely absent in others. The only time of year they seem to consistently pass through the islands (albeit in small numbers) is in May when migrating northward.

Very rare finches

Gray-crowned rosy-finches have been seen on Mt. Constitution on Orcas Island on a couple of occasions, most recently in April 2011 (Barb Jensen, *Tweeters* e-mail report). While the **pine grosbeak** generally stays well above sea level, irregularly they wander to lower altitudes in the winter. Their visits to San Juan Island are unpredictable, but look for them in mixed woods where they have the opportunity to forage on fruits, seeds, and tree buds. The author saw a pair in the scrubby trees near the Cattle Point Lighthouse in February 2009, and a single bird was seen at English Camp in May 2009 (Blake Hough, *eBird*). A pair was also seen at Westside Lake on San Juan Island in February 2010 (Blake Hough, *eBird*). **White-winged crossbills** have been reported twice on Orcas Island in December 1951 and January1980 and once on San Juan Island in April 1986 (Lewis and Sharpe 1987). In May 2011 a pair of **Lawrence's goldfinches** were seen near Friday Harbor; this was the first county record of this species (Barb Jensen, *Tweeters* e-mail report).

Old World Sparrows

House sparrow
Passer domesticus
Common
Year-round
Sites: Friday Harbor, Cattle Point, Roche Harbor
Notes: House sparrows were introduced to North America in the 1850s and started reaching western Washington by the late 1800s. This species thrives in urban habitats, and there have been concerns about house sparrows out-competing cavity-nesting birds in more rural habitats. Interestingly enough, house sparrow numbers have been declining again in recent decades, and the most likely factor is that they are in turn being out-competed by a native species: the house finch. House finches are highly adaptable and expanding in range, and may be causing a decline throughout North America of this non-native species.

Local Bird Conservation Issues

As a wildlife enthusiast with a biology background, I found it impossible to write an account of the birds of San Juan Island without also writing about the threats local species are facing and the important conservation efforts that have occurred in the past or need to occur to ensure their long term survival in the Salish Sea. Every naturalist I spoke to had anecdotes to share recalling species they used to see but no longer do, changes in species abundance, or sightings of new species that never used to occur in San Juan County. These observations relate directly to bird conservation issues, and I have attempted to address the main themes surrounding local bird conservation in the following four sections.

1. Seabird Declines

When you ask local birdwatchers what has changed in the San Juan Islands over the last 20 or 30 years, the biggest difference they report is the decline in the number of seabirds. No longer are there flocks of hundreds of Pacific loons or thousands of common murres in the channels surrounding the islands. Bait balls (also known as bird balls) are large feeding frenzies involving multiple marine bird species, and they are much smaller and less numerous than they used to be. Common terns and the parasitic jaegers that used to harass them are now nearly entirely absent.

Science backs up these anecdotal observations. One study that examined changes in winter marine bird abundance in the Salish Sea from 1975 to 2007 found that 14 of 37 species studied showed significant declines. More remarkably, the declines were spread across taxonomic groups and 11 of the species that declined did so by more than 50% (Bower 2009). No species has declined more than the western grebe, which by some estimates has experienced a local population drop of more than 95%. Other species that showed declines of greater than 50% in this study included the red-throated loon, horned grebe, Brandt's cormorant, greater scaup, black scoter, Bonaparte's gull, marbled murrelet, and common murre.

Reduction in marine bird populations is a worldwide phenomenon. With issues like global climate change, ocean acidification, the occurrence of oil spills, and the amount of functional and derelict fishing gear in the water, it is clear that we have significant problems to address regarding the health of our world's oceans. While locally there are clearly issues with industrial contaminants, over-fishing, and shoreline development, some aspects of the Salish Sea marine ecosystem are surprisingly holding par or even thriving.

Examples of marine life in the region that appear to be thriving are our local seals, sea lions, and humpback whales. Harbor seals in particular, which eat herring and sand lance as well as numerous other fish species, depend on some of the same food sources as many of our marine birds. Humpback whales, which were hunted or otherwise extirpated from the region nearly a century ago, have been re-expanding their range to include inland waters over the last decade. They also eat herring and other small schooling fish. If the food sources are doing well enough to support these marine mammal populations, why are they failing to sustain the loons, murres, and puffins?

One of the main reasons seals are able to thrive when some seabirds are not is because they are generalist feeders, able to opportunistically feed on a wide variety of marine life. If one prey type isn't doing so well, they can more easily turn to another than many sea bird species, which in many cases are more specialists in their feeding habits. Some of the sea birds that are generalists, like the bufflehead, are doing fairly well.

Clearly, sea birds also need more than just a food source to thrive. The ever-increasing human population in the region is one major factor with many direct and indirect effects on seabird populations. Impacts include an increase in the amount of contaminated run-off, loss and/or alteration of nesting and roosting habitat sites, and damage to estuary and river delta habitats.

For nesting seabird species, the introduction of non-native predators, particularly mammals, to islands that act as nest sites can greatly influence nesting success. In addition to preying upon birds and eggs, they also destroy habitat or take over burrows. The iconic tufted puffin is one nesting species that experienced dramatic declines throughout the 1980s and 1990s, and in 2007 and 2008 surveys showed that only about 50% of historic puffin breeding colonies in the state of Washington were still active ("Seabird Ecology" WDFW). Five of the seven historic breeding sites in the inland waters of the Salish Sea were no longer active. Currently it isn't clear what the culprit is for tufted puffin declines in the Salish Sea, though studies are ongoing.

Local fisheries have a large effect on marine bird populations, as well. Even if they're not directly depleting fish species the birds are dependent upon, birds are accidentally caught as bycatch, particularly in gill nets. Birds can also become entangled in lost or damaged nets, lines, and traps that remain in the ecosystem for years or even decades.

There are efforts underway to remove derelict fishing gear, with the Northwest Straits Commission removing more than 870 gillnets from the region since 2002. From what they've found, the effects on San Juan County seabirds are clear. 505 of these 870 nets were in the San Juan Islands, and 14% of these 870 nets held dead marine birds. More than 500 birds of 15 different species were recovered (Good et al. 2009). With the presence of scavengers and the rapid degradation of carcasses underwater, this only represents a small portion of the birds killed by these nets. While the most common birds found in derelict fishing nets were cormorants, loons, and scoters, the above study also reported that the birds most often killed as bycatch in active nets are common murres and rhinoceros auklets.

Since most seabirds are migratory, the issues also span beyond just the Salish Sea. In the case of the western grebe, environmental issues on the freshwater lakes where they breed are likely the main factor in their drastic population drop. While industrial contaminants and oil spills can affect western grebes in marine habitats, wetland degradation and disturbance from human recreation during the breeding season are documented contributors to a reduction in breeding grebe numbers (Bower 2009).

Some species that appear to be experiencing declines actually have stable populations across their entire range and are just shifting their habitat use away from the Salish Sea. One example of this is with brant. Sightings of this sea goose have declined within the Salish Sea, but Christmas Bird Count data show an overall increasing trend in numbers across the continent (Bower 2009). The wintering grounds for this species are altering, leading to a decline of sightings in local waters; this is an example of why a "big picture" approach must be taken even when looking at regional biological phenomena.

The issues influencing local seabird numbers are complex, as evidenced by the increase in some marine bird species as others are experiencing drastic population declines. For example, pigeon guillemots, double-crested cormorants, and pelagic cormorants have shown local increases of more than 50% over the same time period that other species showed greater than 50% declines (Bower 2009). Additionally, there are numerous natural fluctuations in climate, such as La Niña/El Niño events and the Pacific Decadal Oscillation, a climate shift that occurs on the scale of every 20-30 years. These shifts influence temperature and food availability in specific regions over the course of years or even decades, making it an even more daunting task to parse out what is leading to population changes in local bird species.

In 2010 the SeaDoc Society, a local agency that conducts scientific research in the Salish Sea, started a multi-year study to examine the ecosystem-level mechanisms that are driving population changes among local marine birds. Their transboundary effort includes both American and Canadian studies and will help identify some of the main factors influencing specific bird species' population dynamics. The results of this study will be key in directing future actions that need to be taken to help local marine bird populations recover.

2. Shoreline Health

The San Juan Islands don't host large numbers of breeding or over-wintering shorebirds, and play only a minor role as habitat for migrating species. At first it may be somewhat surprising that the San Juan Islands are not a prime shorebird habitat. They are, after all, coastal habitat right in the middle of the Pacific Flyway, and there are several nearby sites – such as Padilla Bay, Skagit Bay, and the Fraser River Delta, that host thousands of shorebirds during migration. Upon closer inspection, however, the San Juan Islands don't have an abundance of sandy beaches or wetland estuaries that are prime stopover sites for shorebirds. Instead, most coastal habitat is rocky shoreline, which makes the islands a good place for black turnstones, wandering tattlers, surfbirds, and rock sandpipers, but the majority of the populations of these species still prefer to travel along the outer coast. The only rocky coastline bird that currently occurs regularly in substantial numbers and is highly dependent on the intertidal habitat in the San Juan Islands is the black oystercatcher. Even though greater shorebird numbers occur elsewhere in the state, local birders have noticed shorebird declines: the flocks of peeps at False Bay are smaller, fewer dunlin overwinter in San Juan Valley, black-bellied plovers occur in smaller numbers, and uncommon species have become even rarer.

Due to the relatively minor role the San Juan Islands play for most shorebirds, conservation and recovery of many species relates to issues beyond the scope of our region. As with any species of concern, there is a long list of factors that are contributing to shorebird declines. Some species used to be hunted, and have not recovered from the impact that sport had on their populations. Invasive species are another major issue, ranging from non-native invertebrates in estuarine habitats that influence prey availability to introduced beach grasses that alter nesting habitat for species like the snowy plover. Plastic in the oceans, oil spills, and contaminants from industry, agriculture, and household use all play a role, as do human disturbance and, most crucially, habitat loss. Due to the fact that shorebirds congregate in large numbers in relatively limited habitats, they are particularly susceptible to habitat degradation. The fact that most species are also long-distance migrants makes developing conservation plans that much more complex because so many different regions are involved. More than 60% of Washington's intertidal wetlands have been destroyed over the last century (Drut and Buchanan 2000). Prairie habitat, which is also used by some shorebird species and used to occur more widely in the Puget Trough, has largely been converted to agricultural lands, been lost to development, or been damaged by invasive species.

Many agencies in the Pacific Northwest are working to address what they can when it comes to helping shorebird populations remain stable or recover. In the year 2000, the North Pacific Regional Working Group operating under the National Shorebird Conservation Plan assessed all 40 shorebird species that occur in western Washington and Oregon and developed a regional conservation plan. Half of all locally occurring shorebird species were identified as being species of regional high concern, including birds like the black oystercatcher, dunlin, greater yellowlegs, and sanderling, which all regularly occur in the San Juan Islands (Drut and Buchanan 2000). The conservation plan laid the groundwork for population assessment and monitoring, management coordination, habitat protection goals, and public education. Dozens of projects that address these issues have been undertaken with efforts by more than 30 different agencies including Oregon and Washington Departments of Fish and Wildlife, four regional universities, The Nature Conservancy, Ducks Unlimited, and Pacific Coast Joint Venture, a group focused on wetland habitat restoration (Thomas et al. 2004).

The shorebird species that has received the most local research attention is the black oystercatcher. The entire global population of the black oystercatcher lives between Alaska and Mexico; at approximately 10,000 birds, it is one of the least abundant shorebird species in North America. About 400 of these birds live year-round in Washington's inland waters. The black oystercatcher is considered a keystone species; they are an indicator of the overall health of the rocky intertidal ecosystem. There are three reasons oystercatchers are a keystone species: their relatively small population size, their dependence on the narrow habitat margin of the rocky coastline, and because of their sensitivity to disruption. Things such as shoreline development, vessel disturbances (high wakes can flood oystercatcher nests), pollution and oil spills, and the presence of non-native predators all negatively impact black oystercatcher populations. It is due to these sensitivities that black oystercatchers no longer inhabit southern and central Puget Sound, where dense human populations and highly developed areas in cities like Seattle have caused too much disturbance for this species (Tessler et al. 2010).

Oystercatcher population surveys have occurred more regularly in the San Juan Islands than elsewhere in the state and have revealed a relatively stable breeding population from the 1970s through the 2000s. It is a positive indicator of regional shoreline health that the local oystercatcher population has remained stable. With monitoring systems and conservation plans in place in Washington and elsewhere throughout shorebird habitat in North America, there is reason to be hopeful that shorebird population declines can be curbed and species can begin to recover.

3. Terrestrial Habitat Changes

The terrestrial habitats seen on San Juan Island today are varied, ranging from suburban town settings to rural farmland and from dense forests to open prairie. Despite being only 55 square miles, a wide diversity of habitat exists here, and human changes to that habitat over the years have led to shifts in the bird species that occur here.

Not long after the glaciers receded at the end of the last ice age, local Native Americans started utilizing the San Juan Islands and surrounding area. The Coast Salish peoples have inhabited the Salish Sea region for at least the last 11,500 years, with archaeological evidence found in the San Juan Islands from 4500 years ago (older evidence of coastal island use may have been destroyed by erosion or tidal action). Interestingly, the earliest documented inhabitants seemed to use mostly terrestrial resources like deer and plants before increasing consumption of marine resources like shellfish and salmon in more recent centuries (Stein 2000). One common practice was harvesting camas bulbs in the spring, after which they would burn the area to boost fertility of the land for the next season. This functioned to help maintain the prairie habitat that covered parts of the San Juans.

Remnants of these prairie habitats still exist, like on the south end of San Juan Island from American Camp to Cattle Point. With a sandy substrate and heavy winds, it doesn't appear that trees have ever grown on this part of the island (Stein 2000). The grasslands found here is prime habitat for bird species like American pipits, short-eared owls, and northern harriers, all species still regularly seen here during the right time of year. Some of the summer breeding species, however, haven't done as well despite the fact that the prairie habitat there is relatively intact. Western meadowlarks and horned larks no longer breed on San Juan Island, while vesper sparrows only occur in very small numbers. These ground nesters have been impacted by another factor: introduced predators, particularly foxes and feral cats.

Garry oak prairie habitats also occurred throughout much of the inland part of the island. Many of the south-facing slopes throughout the archipelago are more barren than the heavily forested northern sides due in part to most of the wind and sun coming from the south. Most of these drier slopes were historically Garry oak habitat. One prime example in San Juan Valley is the south-facing slope of Mt. Young. During the time of English occupation at British Camp in the 1860s, there were more than 100 acres of Garry Oak habitat in that part of the island ("SJI NHP – Garry Oak", 2011) These trees thrive in the slightly drier climate found in the rainshadow east of the Olympic Mountains, including the San Juan Islands. More than 100 bird species including warblers, vireos, woodpeckers, and swallows have been found associated with Garry oak ecosystems in western North America. They utilize nesting cavities, acorns, dead wood, insects, and shelter related to the trees (Fuchs 2001).

With extensive European settlement starting about 150 years ago, this part of the local ecosystem started to change. The settler population of San Juan Island exploded from 45 to 3500 between 1860 and 1900 (Vouri and Vouri 2010). Around the turn of the century, focus shifted from homesteading to more commercial ventures like agriculture, fishing, and the lime industry, and this took its toll on the habitat. Development associated with population growth and the advent of the above industries destroyed Garry oak habitat, and fire suppression led to Douglas fir forests encroaching on these areas and shading out the oaks and the grassland understory.

The invasion of the introduced European starling, which aggressively out-competes many native species for nesting sites, contributed to the decline in the 1960s and 70s of many cavity-nesting species linked with the deteriorating Garry oak habitat. The western bluebird was locally extirpated due to these factors. Other local bird species that in some regions are heavily associated with Garry oaks include western screech-owls, downy woodpeckers, band-tailed pigeons, Wilson's and orange-crowned warblers, and chipping sparrows. Many of these species have also experienced downward population trends in the region (Fuchs 2001).

While the European starling has impacted cavity-nesting bird species in Garry oak habitats on the island, another newly arrived species is having impacts of its own on local nesters: the brown-headed cowbird. The story is that brown-headed cowbirds were historically associated with the buffalo of the plains, where they would feed on insects kicked up by the herds. Since they followed the herds, they were unable to stay in a nesting site for the duration of the breeding season, and thus evolved to be brood parasites, which is to say that they lay their eggs in nests of other bird species, leaving their chicks to be raised by unsuspecting foster parents. A single female cowbird can parasitize up to 30-40 nests in a breeding season (Petit 2011). Sometimes she removes eggs of native birds, while in other cases chicks out-compete native nestlings for food or even push them out of the nest.

Some bird species that lived in the plains with cowbirds have adapted mechanisms to resist cowbird brood parasitism, either by recognizing cowbird eggs and discarding them, building another nest if a cowbird egg is found, or raising multiple broods over the course of a breeding season, only one of which is likely to be parasitized during the relatively short cowbird breeding season. Problems have arisen within the last century or so, however, as logging and the spread of agriculture have created more cowbird habitat across the country, allowing them to expand well beyond their native range of the Great Plains. This has introduced cowbird brood parasitism to numerous bird species that have had no time to adapt a mechanism to avoid it, and thus cowbirds are a factor contributing to the declines of many species such as numerous warblers and vireos. Since cowbirds thrive in rural habitats, population control is difficult; the best option to aid many native bird species is to preserve large patches of forest which cowbirds are reluctant to penetrate.

Garry oak habitat restoration efforts are underway throughout the region, including in the San Juan Islands. A part of many restoration plans is prescribed burns, an element that was a regular part of the ecosystem due both to lightning strikes and the landscape management efforts of native peoples. Fire tolerant bark helps adult Garry oaks survive fires, while saplings have deep roots and the ability to re-sprout if destroyed. Other woodland species like Douglas fir tend to be kept at bay by regular fires. Prescribed burns also help eliminate invasive herbaceous species, further restoring local habitats (Fuchs 2001). Burns have been underway on Mt. Young in British Camp since 2003 ("SJI NHP – Garry Oak", 2011). In some areas, instead of fires, cutting and manual removal occurs to help the understory grasses regain a foothold in the ecosystem.

Forest habitat, like prairie habitat, has been altered on the island as well. Logging has had major impacts to woodland habitats in the San Juan Islands. Prior to European settlement, much of the islands were covered with old growth forest, prime habitat for species like northern goshawks, spotted owls, and even nesting marbled murrelets. These forests were logged between the 1860s and 1950s. Many trees were used for timber, and more went to fuel the local lime kiln industry. While local legend claims that most of the trees in the county were felled to serve as fuel for the lime kilns, in actuality it was probably closer to 10% of the forests that were logged for this purpose (Schroeder 2011). Still, this resulted in fragmenting the old growth forest habitat and fundamentally altering the forest structure. While many houses on the island are tucked away among the trees, the building of them still served to break apart the forest and disrupt the presence of species that prefer large uninhabited territories, like the great horned owl. A large contiguous patch of old growth forest in the county is preserved in Moran State Park on Orcas Island. The dense forest of Moran State Park also includes the highest elevations in the San Juan Islands on Mt. Constitution, and this combination of old growth forest and altitude leads to some unique birds like sooty grouse, gray-crowned rosy finches, and Clark's nutcrackers occasionally appearing here and no where else in the county.

4. Successful Stories

With many big conservation concerns facing both marine and terrestrial birds in the San Juan Islands, it is helpful to draw strength from some of the major bird recovery efforts that have been successful. One of the most significant stories, on both a national and regional level, is that of the bald eagle.

Despite being adopted as our national symbol in 1782, the bald eagle was long a misunderstood bird. Many farmers and ranchers routinely shot eagles that they believed fed on their livestock and other domesticated animals, while in fact eagles primarily eat fish and seabirds and generally only feed on mammals when they're found as carrion. In 1940, the Bald and Golden Eagle

Protection Act was signed into law, making it illegal to kill or take any part of a bald eagle, its nest, or its eggs.

While the new Eagle Protection Act gave bald eagles security against poaching, another event of the same decade nearly spelled their demise. Today, it's a little hard to believe that in the 1940s the discovery of DDT and its use as a pesticide was so celebrated that the man who synthesized it won the Nobel Prize. One of the slew of insecticides released after World War II and its research regarding chemical warfare, DDT was hailed as being an environmentally safe method of killing insects on crops. In the 1950s and 1960s, however, after DDT had been running into the waterways for more than a decade, the true effects began to be realized. Bald eagles, peregrine falcons, and brown pelicans were among the species experiencing dramatic population declines due to eggshell thinning caused by DDT.

In 1967, bald eagles south of the 40th parallel in the continental United States were listed as endangered under the Endangered Species Preservation Act. In 1972, after the detrimental effects of DDT on both wildlife and human health had been demonstrated through works like Rachel Carson's revolutionary book Silent Spring, the Environmental Protection Agency took a step that was controversial at the time and banned the use of DDT in the United States. The modern Endangered Species Act (ESA) was created in 1973, and in 1978 the bald eagle was listed as endangered in 43 of the lower 48 states and listed as threatened in the other five states, including Washington.

Some of the first surveys of nesting bald eagles in Washington were centered in the San Juan Islands. The first local survey was in 1962 when five nests were found in the county (Stinson et al. 2001); at this time there were thought to be fewer than 500 nesting pairs across the continental United States ("Bald Eagle Recovery" 2010). After the banning of DDT and the additional protection afforded by the ESA, the eagle population immediately began to recover. In 1995, the same year the bald eagle was downgraded to a threatened listing on the ESA in all of the contiguous United States, there were 102 nests found in San Juan County (Stinson et al. 2001).

By 1999, the bald eagle had recovered sufficiently enough across the country that there was talk of de-listing it from the Endangered Species Act entirely. This eventually happened in the summer of 2007, when there were more than 10,000 known nesting sites in the Lower 48 ("Bald Eagle Recovery" 2010). There are currently more than 125 nesting pairs in San Juan County ("San Juan NHP – Birds" 2010).

The banning of DDT and an Endangered Species Act listing similarly combined to help the recovery of peregrine falcons and brown pelicans. Peregrine falcons, which also benefited from a captive breeding and release program, were de-listed from the ESA in 1999. Numbers in Washington went from five breeding pairs in 1980 to more than 70 in 2001. The San Juan Islands are one of the most concentrated breeding areas in the state, and numbers here went from two breeding pairs 1980 to 21 in 2001 (Hayes and Buchanan 2002). The brown pelican, which initially received federal protection in 1969 and was immediately listed on the ESA when it passed in 1973, was also de-listed in 2009.

With toxic chemicals like PCBs and PBDEs now receiving attention for their effects on the health of local marine wildlife, we can find encouragement and reasons for hope in the successful recovery of these three bird species following the banning of DDT.

*   *   *

Another local recovery story is the success of the reintroduction of the western bluebird. This native species was extirpated from the San Juan Islands during the 1960s due to the arrival of the European starling and loss of Garry oak habitat. Seven organizations including the San Juan Preservation Trust combined to start the Western Bluebird Reintroduction Project in 2007 that was modeled after successful reintroduction efforts that have taken place across the country. For five years, pairs were relocated from a healthy bluebird population at Fort Lewis near

Olympia to San Juan Island. After being released, pairs effectively nested in increasing numbers every year, and individuals have continued to return to the island every spring of their own accord, indicating that the population has been successfully reestablished in the county. In 2010, twelve breeding pairs fledged 84 young on San Juan Island, and in 2011 a nesting pair was found on Lopez Island as well (Kathleen Foley, pers. comm.).

*   *   *

When Seattle mayor Robert Moran donated more than 5000 acres on Orcas Island to what would become Moran State Park in 1921, he set the precedence for the San Juan Islands being one of the state and national leaders in conservation issues over the next century. Today, San Juan County is home to the San Juan National Historical Park, the San Juan Islands National Wildlife Refuge, four Washington State Parks, and 17 county parks. In addition, there are several local organizations with missions to protect regional ecosystems. The San Juan Preservation Trust, founded in 1979, was the first non-profit land trust formed in Washington. It strives "to preserve and protect open spaces, scenic views, forests, agricultural lands, habitats, watersheds, riparian corridors, wetlands, and shorelines in the San Juan Archipelago". The San Juan County Land Bank, formed in 1990 when voters passed legislation to exercise a real estate excise tax, has the goal "to preserve in perpetuity areas in the County that have environmental, agricultural, aesthetic, cultural, scientific, historic, scenic, or low-intensity recreational value, and to protect existing and future sources of potable water". Both these organizations are active in acquiring and maintaining land for conservation purposes, which benefits many aspects of San Juan Island, bird life included. Their work is supported and supplemented by the efforts of numerous other local organizations dedicated to conservation, wildlife management, and environmental education including the SeaDoc Society, the Marine Resources Committee, the San Juan Nature Institute, the Salish Sea Association of Marine Naturalists, Friends of the San

Juan Islands, and People for Puget Sound. As one San Juan Island resident put it, "It is remarkable to live in a community that values the natural world."

As with wildlife everywhere, there are some major issues surrounding human influences on both marine and terrestrial habitats in the Salish Sea that need to be carefully monitored and addressed to ensure our local bird life recovers and continues to thrive. With stories like that of the bald eagle and western bluebird, there is reason to hope that other species such as the western grebe and horned lark can also make local recoveries. With the right combination of science, management, advocacy and legislation ecosystems can successfully be preserved and restored to benefit our avian friends. It is the role of the bird enthusiast, like yourself, to get out and enjoy the amazing variety of species we have on San Juan Island, and to share your sightings and spread your passion for local wildlife with others.

Additional Resources

San Juan Island Trails Committee
www.sanjuanislandtrails.org
360-378-4953

Island Rec, the local park and recreation district, created the Trails Committee in 1999 to promote, build, and maintain the trail system on San Juan Island. They work with other local organizations and are active in generating new trails on the island. Their website includes great maps of many trail sites and is also worth checking out to see if any new trails have opened since the publication of this book.

Wolf Hollow Wildlife Rehabilitation Center
www.wolfhollowwildlife.org
360-378-5000

Wolf Hollow is the local wildlife rescue facility that cares for injured animals. If, during your bird-watching adventures, you come across an injured bird or other animal they are the ones to contact at the above phone number. Staff members are on call 24 hours a day.

The San Juan Preservation Trust Bluebird Reintroduction Project
www.sjpt.org
360-378-2461

The Preservation Trust is the local organization responsible for the western bluebird reintroduction project. They collect sightings of western bluebirds in the San Juan Islands.

San Juan Islands Marine Mammal Stranding Network
www.whalemuseum.com/programs/mmsn
1-800-562-8832

The local stranding network is a program of The Whale Museum that collects data on live and dead stranded marine mammals of all species. If you come across an injured or dead marine mammal on any San Juan beaches, please report it to the above phone number. The same number also functions as a marine mammal sightings hotline, and they are always interested in your reports of live marine mammals as well.

Bibliography

Aanerud, Kevin. "Fifth Report of the WBRC". *Washington Birds* 8 (2002): 1-18. PDF file.

Aanerud, Kevin, and Philip W. Mattocks, Jr. "Fourth Report of the WBRC". *Washington Birds* 7 (2000): 7-24. PDF file.

---. "Third Report of the WBRC". *Washington Birds* 6 (1997): 7-31. PDF file.

"Bald Eagle Recovery". U.S. Fish and Wildlife Service. August 2010. Web. Accessed May 2011.

Baron, Nancy, and John Acorn. *Birds of the Pacific Northwest Coast.* Renton, WA: Lone Pine Publishing, 1997. Print.

Bartels, Matt (Ed.). "San Juan County". *Washington Birder County Firsts.* 2010. PDF file.

Bartels, Matt (Ed.). *Washington Cumulative County Yearlist Project.* Washington Birder. Web. Accessed October 2010-April 2011.

Baughman, Mel. *National Geographic Atlas to the Birds of North America.* Washington, DC: National Geographic Society, 2003. Print.

Bird Web. Seattle Audubon Society. Web. Accessed October 2010-June 2011.

Bower, John. "Changes in Marine Bird Abundance in the Salish Sea From 1975-2007". *Marine Ornithology* 37 (2009): 9-17. PDF file.

Breeding Bird Atlas Explorer. US Geological Survey Patuxent Wildlife Research Center & National Biological Information Infrastructure. 2011. Web. Accessed March 2011. Data extracted from: Smith, M.R., P.W. Mattocks, Jr., and K.M. Cassidy. 1997. *Breeding Birds of Washington State.* Volume 4 in Washington State Gap Analysis- Final Report (K. M. Cassidy, C.E. Grue, M.R. Smith, and K.M. Dvornich, eds.). Seattle Audubon Society Publications in Zoology No. 1, Seattle, 538 pp.

Contreras, Alan. *Northwest Birds in Winter.* Corvallis, OR: Oregon State University Press, 1997. Print.

Drut, Martin S. and Joseph B. Buchanan. "North Pacific Coast Regional Shorebird Management Plan". US Fish and Wildlife Service and Cascadia Research Collective. 2000. Microsoft Word file.

eBird: An online database of bird distribution and abundance. Cornell Lab of Ornithology and National Aubudon Society. Version 2, 2010. Web. Accessed October 2010 – April 2011.

Fuchs, Marilyn A. "Towards a Recovery Strategy for Garry Oak and Associated Ecosystem in Canada: Ecological Assessment and Literature Review". Technical Report GBEI/EC-00-030. Environment Canada. 2001. PDF file.

Gill, F., and D. Donsker (Eds.). *IOC World Bird Names.* Version 2.7, 2010. Web. Accessed February-July 2011.

Good, Thomas P., et al. "Ghosts of the Salish Sea: Threats to Marine Birds in Puget Sound and the Northwest Straits from Derelict Fishing Gear". *Marine Ornithology* 37 (2009): 67-76. PDF file.

Hayes, G. E. and J.B. Buchanan. "Washington State status report for the Peregrine Falcon" Washington Department of Fish and Wildlife. (2002) 77 pp. PDF file.

Lewis, Mark G., and Fred A. Sharpe. *Birding in the San Juan Islands.* Seattle, WA: The Mountaineers, 1987. Print.

Mlodinow, Steven G. and Kevin Aanerod. "Seventh Report of the WBRC". *Washington Birds* 10 (2008): 21-47. PDF file.

---. "Sixth Report of the WBRC". *Washington Birds* 9 (2006): 39-54. PDF file.

National Geographic Field Guide to the Birds of North America. 4th ed. Washington, DC: National Geographic Society, 2002. Print.

Opperman, Hal. *A Birder's Guide to Washington.* Colorado Springs, CO: American Birding Association, Inc., 2003. Print.

Petit, Lisa. "Brown-Headed Cowbirds: From Buffalo Birds to Modern Scourge". Smithsonian Migratory Bird Center. Web. Accessed May 2011.

Poole, A. (Ed.). *The Birds of North America Online*. Cornell Lab of Ornithology. Web. Accessed February-March 2011.

"San Juan National Historical Park - Birds". U.S. National Park Service. 2010. Web. Accessed February-May 2011.

"San Juan National Historic park – Garry Oak". US National Park Service. 2001. Web. Accessed May 2011.

Schroeder, Tom. "The Lime Industry and Timber Cutting: A Quantitative Analysis". Forest Info. Web. Accessed May 2011.

"Seabird Ecology". Washington Department of Fish and Wildlife. Web. Accessed February-May 2011.

Siegel, Rodney B., Robert L. Wilkerson, and Heidi K. Pedersen. "Landbird Inventory of San Juan Island National Historical Park". The Institute for Bird Populations, 2002. PDF file.

Stein, Julie K. *Exploring Coast Salish Prehistory: The Archaeology of San Juan Island*. Seattle, WA: University of Washington Press, 2000. Print.

Stinson, D.W., J.W. Watson, and K.R. McAllister. "Washington state status report for the bald eagle". Washington Department of Fish and Wildlife. (2001) 92 pp. PDF file.

Tessler, D.F., et al. "Black Oystercatcher Conservation Action Plan". Version 1.1. Alaska Department of Fish and Game and US Fish and Wildlife Service. (2010) 115 pp. PDF file.

The Christmas Bird Count Historical Results. National Audubon Society. Web. Accessed October 2010-April 2011.

Thomas, Sue, Ruth Milner, and Joe Buchanan. "Summaries of current projects that benefit shorebirds in the coastal region of Oregon and Washington." US Fish and Wildlife Service. (2004) 30 pp. PDF file.

Tweit, Bill, and Dennis Paulson. "First Report of the WBRC". *Washington Birds* 3 (1994): 11-41. PDF file.

Tweit, Bill, and Jeff Skriletz. "Second Report of the WBRC". *Washington Birds* 5 (1996): 7-28. PDF file.

Vernon, Susan. *Rainshadow World: A Naturalist's Year in the San Juan Islands.* Friday Harbor, WA: Archipelago Press, 2010. Print.

Vouri, Mike, and Julia Vouri. *Images of America: San Juan Island.* Charleston, South Carolina: Arcadia Publishing, 2010. Print.

Wahl, Terrence R., Bill Tweit, and Steven G. Mlodinow. *Birds of Washington: Status and Distribution.* Corvallis, OR: Oregon State University Press, 2005. Print.

Williams, Hill. *The Restless Northwest: A Geological Story.* Pullman, WA: Washington State University Press, 2002. Print.

WOS News. Issues 18-123. Washington Ornithological Society. April 1992 – November 2009. PDF files.

San Juan County Checklist

Species are listed in taxonomic order with the exception of the very rare species, which are listed at the end of their taxonomic section in italics

Geese and Swans

- ☐ Greater white-fronted goose
- ☐ Brant
- ☐ Cackling goose
- ☐ Canada goose
- ☐ Mute swan
- ☐ Trumpeter swan
- ☐ Tundra swan

Ducks

- ☐ Wood duck
- ☐ Gadwall
- ☐ Eurasian wigeon
- ☐ American wigeon
- ☐ Mallard
- ☐ Blue-winged teal
- ☐ Cinnamon teal
- ☐ Northern shoveler
- ☐ Northern pintail
- ☐ Green-winged teal
- ☐ Canvasback
- ☐ Ring-necked duck
- ☐ Greater scaup
- ☐ Lesser scaup
- ☐ Harlequin duck
- ☐ Surf scoter
- ☐ White-winged scoter
- ☐ Black scoter
- ☐ Long-tailed duck
- ☐ Bufflehead
- ☐ Common goldeneye
- ☐ Barrow's goldeneye
- ☐ Hooded merganser
- ☐ Common merganser
- ☐ Red-breasted merganser
- ☐ Ruddy duck
- ☐ *Common teal*
- ☐ *Redhead*
- ☐ *Tufted duck*
- ☐ *King eider*

Pheasants and Quail

- ☐ California quail
- ☐ Ring-necked pheasant
- ☐ Wild turkey
- ☐ *Ruffed grouse*
- ☐ *Sooty grouse*

Loons

☐ Red-throated loon
☐ Pacific loon
☐ Common loon
☐ *Arctic loon*
☐ *Yellow-billed loon*

Grebes

☐ Pied-billed grebe
☐ Horned grebe
☐ Red-necked grebe
☐ Eared grebe
☐ Western grebe
☐ Clark's grebe

Tubenoses

☐ Sooty shearwater
☐ *Black-footed albatross*
☐ *Northern fulmar*
☐ *Pink-footed shearwater*
☐ *Short-tailed shearwater*
☐ *Manx shearwater*
☐ *Fork-tailed storm-petrel*
☐ *Leach's storm-petrel*

Cormorants

☐ Brandt's cormorant
☐ Double-crested cormorant
☐ Pelagic cormorant
☐ *Brown booby*

Pelicans

☐ American white pelican
☐ Brown pelican

Herons

☐ Great blue heron
☐ Green heron
☐ *American bittern*
☐ *Great egret*
☐ *Black-crowned night heron*

Raptors

☐ Turkey vulture
☐ Osprey
☐ Bald eagle
☐ Northern harrier
☐ Sharp-shinned hawk
☐ Cooper's hawk
☐ Red-tailed hawk
☐ Rough-legged hawk
☐ Golden eagle
☐ American kestrel
☐ Merlin
☐ Peregrine falcon
☐ *Gyrfalcon*
☐ *Northern goshawk*
☐ *Swainson's hawk*
☐ *Ferruginous hawk*
☐ *Prairie falcon*

Rails and Cranes

☐ Virginia rail
☐ Sora
☐ American coot
☐ *Sandhill crane*

Shorebirds

☐ Black-bellied plover
☐ Semipalmated plover
☐ Killdeer
☐ Black oystercatcher
☐ Spotted sandpiper
☐ Wandering tattler
☐ Greater yellowlegs
☐ Lesser yellowlegs
☐ Whimbrel
☐ Ruddy turnstone
☐ Black turnstone
☐ Surfbird
☐ Sanderling
☐ Dunlin
☐ Semipalmated sandpiper
☐ Western sandpiper
☐ Least sandpiper
☐ Short-billed dowitcher
☐ Long-billed dowitcher
☐ Wilson's snipe
☐ Wilson's phalarope
☐ Red-necked phalarope
☐ Red phalarope
☐ *American golden plover*
☐ *Pacific golden plover*

☐ *American avocet*
☐ *Solitary sandpiper*
☐ *Willet*
☐ *Long-billed curlew*
☐ *Marbled godwit*
☐ *Red knot*
☐ *Baird's sandpiper*
☐ *Pectoral sandpiper*
☐ *Sharp-tailed sandpiper*
☐ *Rock sandpiper*
☐ *Stilt sandpiper*
☐ *Buff-breasted sandpiper*

Gulls

☐ Black-legged kittiwake
☐ Sabine's gull
☐ Bonaparte's gull
☐ Heermann's gull
☐ Mew gull
☐ Ring-billed gull
☐ Western gull
☐ California gull
☐ Herring gull
☐ Thayer's gull
☐ Glaucous-winged gull
☐ *Black-headed gull*
☐ *Little gull*
☐ *Franklin's gull*
☐ *Glaucous gull*

Terns and Jaegers

☐ Caspian tern
☐ Common tern
☐ Parasitic jaeger
☐ *Black tern*
☐ *Arctic tern*
☐ *Elegant tern*
☐ *Pomarine jaeger*
☐ *Long-tailed jaeger*

Alcids

☐ Common murre
☐ Pigeon guillemot
☐ Marbled murrelet
☐ Ancient murrelet
☐ Cassin's auklet
☐ Rhinoceros auklet
☐ Tufted puffin
☐ *Thick-billed murre*
☐ *Long-billed murrelet*
☐ *Kittlitz's murrelet*

Pigeons and Doves

☐ Rock pigeon
☐ Band-tailed pigeon
☐ Eurasian collared-dove
☐ Mourning dove

Owls

☐ Barn owl
☐ Western screech-owl
☐ Great horned owl
☐ Snowy owl
☐ Barred owl
☐ Short-eared owl
☐ Northern saw-whet owl
☐ *Northern pygmy-owl*
☐ *Burrowing owl*
☐ *Spotted owl*
☐ *Long-eared owl*

Nighthawks and Swifts

☐ Common nighthawk
☐ Black swift
☐ Vaux's swift

Hummingbirds

☐ Anna's hummingbird
☐ Rufous hummingbird

Kingfishers

☐ Belted kingfisher

Woodpeckers

☐ Red-breasted sapsucker
☐ Downy woodpecker
☐ Hairy woodpecker

☐ Northern flicker
☐ Pileated woodpecker
☐ Lewis' woodpecker
☐ *Red-naped sapsucker*
☐ *White-headed woodpecker*

Flycatchers

☐ Olive-sided flycatcher
☐ Western wood-pewee
☐ Willow flycatcher
☐ Hammond's flycatcher
☐ Pacific-slope flycatcher
☐ Western kingbird
☐ *Dusky flycatcher*
☐ *Say's phoebe*
☐ *Ash-throated flycatcher*
☐ *Eastern kingbird*

Shrikes

☐ Northern shrike

Vireos

☐ Cassin's vireo
☐ Hutton's vireo
☐ Warbling vireo
☐ *Red-eyed vireo*

Corvids

☐ Northwestern crow
☐ Common raven

☐ Steller's jay
☐ *Blue jay*
☐ *Gray jay*
☐ *Clark's nutcracker*
☐ *Black-billed magpie*

Larks and Swallows

☐ Horned lark
☐ Purple martin
☐ Tree swallow
☐ Violet-green swallow
☐ Northern rough-winged swallow
☐ Cliff swallow
☐ Barn swallow
☐ *Eurasian skylark*
☐ *Bank swallow*

Chickadees, Bushtits, Creepers, and Nuthatches

☐ Chestnut-backed chickadee
☐ Bushtit
☐ Red-breasted nuthatch
☐ Brown creeper
☐ *Black-capped chickadee*

Wrens and Dippers

☐ Bewick's wren
☐ House wren
☐ Pacific wren

☐ Marsh wren
☐ *Rock wren*
☐ *American dipper*

Kinglets

☐ Golden-crowned kinglet
☐ Ruby-crowned kinglet

Thrushes and Thrashers

☐ Western bluebird
☐ Mountain bluebird
☐ Townsend's solitaire
☐ Swainson's thrush
☐ Hermit thrush
☐ American robin
☐ Varied thrush
☐ *Brown thrasher*

Starlings

☐ European starling

Pipits and Accentors

☐ American pipit
☐ *Siberian accentor*
☐ *Red-throated pipit*

Waxwings

☐ Cedar waxwing
☐ *Bohemian waxwing*

Longspurs and Buntings

☐ Lapland longspur
☐ Snow bunting

Warblers

☐ Orange-crowned warbler
☐ Yellow warbler
☐ Yellow-rumped warbler
☐ Black-throated gray warbler
☐ Townsend's warbler
☐ MacGillivray's warbler
☐ Common yellowthroat
☐ Wilson's warbler
☐ *Tennessee warbler*
☐ *Hermit warbler*
☐ *Palm warbler*
☐ *Black-and-white warbler*
☐ *Ovenbird*

Sparrows

☐ Spotted towhee
☐ Chipping sparrow
☐ Vesper sparrow
☐ Savannah sparrow
☐ Fox sparrow
☐ Song sparrow
☐ Lincoln's sparrow
☐ White-throated sparrow
☐ White-crowned sparrow
☐ Golden-crowned sparrow
☐ Dark-eyed junco

☐ American tree sparrow
☐ Lark sparrow
☐ Clay-colored sparrow
☐ Black-throated sparrow

Tanagers and Grosbeaks

☐ Western tanager
☐ Black-headed grosbeak
☐ Lazuli bunting
☐ Rose-breasted grosbeak
☐ Indigo bunting

Blackbirds and Orioles

☐ Red-winged blackbird
☐ Western meadowlark
☐ Brewer's blackbird
☐ Brown-headed cowbird
☐ Bobolink
☐ Yellow-headed blackbird
☐ Bullock's oriole

Finches

☐ Purple finch
☐ House finch
☐ Red crossbill
☐ Pine siskin
☐ American goldfinch
☐ Evening grosbeak
☐ Gray-crowned rosy-finch
☐ Pine grosbeak
☐ White-winged crossbill

☐ Lawrence's goldfinch

Old World Sparrows

☐ House sparrow

Additional Sightings

☐
☐
☐
☐
☐

CPSIA information can be obtained at www.ICGtesting.com
Printed in the USA
BVOW042325141111

275983BV00001BA/6/P